Preface

Thank you for choosing this textbook for your studies in the English language and about the UK.

The content of the book  ultural issues in Britain. The information prov   from academic and government studies a   l opinions from British people. This approach aims to give   rounded view of the situation in Britain today. It may challenge some stereotypical ideas that you may have about the UK.

Each chapter contains two texts. One of these will usually be more difficult and the other easier; this could be because of the content or the level of English. These differences will give you a different viewpoint on the same theme and are designed to provide you with food for thought and a basis for further study.

As a reading textbook, it provides a vocabulary exercise at the beginning of the first text, followed by two pre-reading questions. Then after the text there are seven multiple choice and three true/false comprehension questions, ending with two writing questions. The second text has five listening questions instead of the vocabulary exercise. The writing questions could also be used as the basis for discussion activities, if needed.

The themes of the book cover a wide range of topics from food to Brexit. We hope you enjoy the variety and will learn a lot more English and more about Britain.

Finally, we would like to thank Shohakusha for giving us the chance to publish this book and to the editorial team including Yukiko Mori and Keiko Nagano.

Modern Britain:
Culture, Society and History

Contents

Castle Park, Colchester, Essex–A muslim women in a burkha, hijab walking with her child in Colchester Castle Park, Essex.

Chapter *1*

Multi-Cultural UK

多文化の国、英国

> 英国内で白人の数が減少している。北部のある地域ではアジア人が人口の大半を占める。人種の混じったコミュニティを推進することが政府に求められる。移民の流入を心配する声もある。仕事や社会保障を求めてアフリカなどから入ってくる移民の権利を守ることは急務なのだ。

Reading 1 ▸ Warm-up

Using your dictionary, find the meanings of the following words.

1. population   2. cohesion   3. intervene   4. ethnic

5. segregated   6. butcher   7. deliberately   8. mosque

Choose the best answer (a-c).

1. 'White flight' means...
   a. white bread that has been fried.
   b. a white coloured plane.
   c. white people leaving an area.

2. Multi-culture refers to...
   a. many cultures.
   b. people of high and low culture.
   c. a lot of people who love culture.

Audio 02

1 The number of white British people living in towns and cities in the UK is getting smaller and in some cases has fallen by 50%, a recent report states.

2 In 2001, in an area of east London called Newham, the population was 33 percent white but ten years later fell to 16 percent.

3 A government adviser for community cohesion says that by 2021 this population imbalance will be even greater. He suggests the government should intervene to make sure there is an ethnic balance in such areas.

4 One city in the north of England called Blackburn is one of the most segregated places in Britain where one area is now 95 percent Asian. The local butcher, an Asian, admits he has never served a white Briton.

5 He says, 'It is not good that we all live separately but how can we fix this problem? Asian families like to live in the same area as each other so we can support one another, but then the white people move out. It's not that we deliberately choose to live separately – it is just what happens. We want to live in this area because we are close to the mosques and all our families are very close to each other.'

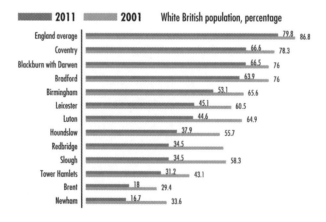

6 The research, published by Open Democracy, calls on the Government to do more to promote mixed communities, especially in light of the spike in hate crime reported since the Brexit referendum.

7 The report says that if people of different cultures contact each other it reduces prejudice and intolerance.

NOTES l. 7: **imbalance** 不均衡、バランスの悪さ l. 12: **fix**〔問題などを〕解決する l. 20: **referendum** 国民投票 l. 22: **prejudice** 偏見 l. 22: **intolerance** 不寛容

Comprehension Questions

Choose the best answer (a-c).

1. According to a recent Open Democracy report, what are white British people in some areas of the UK doing?
   a. Greater numbers are leaving the UK.
   b. A lot of them are leaving those areas.
   c. They are mixing with Asian immigrants.

2. Look at the chart. Which area shows that the white British population has fallen by over half?
   a. Slough
   b. Luton
   c. Newham

3. What does a government adviser warn?
   a. The problem will get worse.
   b. There will be fewer immigrants in future.
   c. The situation will not change.

4. What does the butcher in Blackburn say about white British people?
   a. They don't like buying meat.
   b. They refuse to go to his shop.
   c. They don't live in the area.

5. What does he say about solving the problem?
   a. He doesn't know how to solve it.
   b. He thinks the government should do more.
   c. He doesn't think there is a problem.

6. According to the butcher what are the reasons for Asians living together in certain areas?
   a. They think white British people are dangerous.
   b. They want to help each other.
   c. They want to live in cheap areas of town.

7. Open Democracy would like the government to...
   a. pay money to white people to stay in those areas.
   b. make hatred a crime in the UK.
   c. encourage people to mix together.

T/F Questions

Circle T or F for each of the following statements.

1. White people are leaving certain areas of cities and towns in the UK in significant numbers. (**T** / **F**)

2. One adviser to the government reports that nothing can be done in such areas. (**T** / **F**)

3. Since Brexit racial tolerance has improved in the UK. (**T** / **F**)

Writing Questions

Make a full sentence, using the following words.

1. The problem of (difficult / the government / 'white flight' / for / is / to solve).

   _____

2. Some cities in the (have areas / highly segregated / north of England / which / are).

   _____

© Nicolas Economou

Listening

Listen to the following 'Reading 2'. Fill in the correct phrase in each blank (a-e) and match the definitions below.

a. _____ b. _____ c. _____

d. _____ e. _____

1. dropped to...
2. a large number rushing in
3. money paid each week
4. government help given to needy people
5. a public issue that makes people anxious
6. to look for something
7. number of births

BEST UK
IMMIGRATION SERVICE

Refused
a UK visa?

Reading 2   Fear of Increasing Immigration

1 There are few topics that are more **(a)** than immigration. However, most economists agree that immigrants don't take jobs, nor do they have much impact on wages. Look at the UK, where there are continuing high levels of immigration while unemployment has **(b)** its lowest level in 40 years. More importantly, immigration makes economies more dynamic 5 and is generally positive for productivity and prosperity.

2 The number of people seeking to move countries will continue to grow. This is because of demographics. Every country in Europe has a **(c)** below replacement level. However, the population in developing countries, especially in Africa, is increasing. Not only the UK but also 10 Japan needs to liberalize its immigration policy.

3 Considering these facts, how can we explain the recent extreme political reaction against immigration? During the Brexit campaign in the UK, leavers emphasized the dangers of EU free movement, which is mostly by white Eastern Europeans. But the Brexit campaigners warned 15 of a **(d)** of Asian and black immigrants. Also, some influential people in Britain think that only white people can be "really" British, and that black or Asian Britons are somehow alien and dangerous.

4 Perhaps it is time for politicians to argue for a liberal immigration
20 policy not only on economic grounds but also to defend the rights of
immigrants. The government could also improve health and (e) in areas
of the UK suffering under population pressure.

5 British people need to think again about their attitudes to
immigration and immigrants. Immigration is a social problem and
25 immigrants are people.

NOTES   l. 3: **wage** 〔労働者に支払う〕賃金、時間給   l. 6: **prosperity** 繁栄   l. 11: **liberalize** 〔規制などを〕
緩和する   l. 14: **emphasize** 〔重要性などを〕強調する

Comprehension Questions

Choose the best answer (a-c).

1. What is the writer's main argument about immigration?
   a. It is going to happen, so nothing can be done.
   b. It does not badly affect the economy.
   c. It increases the risk of crime in certain areas.

2. What has happened at the same time as high levels of immigration in the UK?
   a. Wages have not gone down.
   b. The economy has not improved.
   c. British people have welcomed immigrants.

3. Why does the writer predict migration will grow in the future?
   a. Because the population in Europe is decreasing.
   b. Because the economies of developing countries are improving.
   c. Because African countries can get money by sending citizens abroad.

4. What do some important British people think about non-white Britons?
   a. They commit crimes and increase hate.
   b. They are useful for doing low level jobs.
   c. They can never be fully British.

5. How has the Brexit debate affected the chance for a better solution to the immigration issue?
   a. It has increased understanding of the problem.
   b. It has made the possibility less likely.
   c. It has made it possible for more immigration from the EU.

6. According to the writer what should politicians do about immigration?
   a. They should make laws to reduce the numbers of immigrants.
   b. They should persuade white British people to live abroad.
   c. They should open up the country to allow more immigration.

7. How can politicians help in areas of the country where there are a lot of immigrants?
   a. They could provide more social support.
   b. They could separate the immigrants into other areas.
   c. They could encourage people to live apart.

T/F Questions

Circle T or F for each of the following statements.

1. Immigration is one of the least emotional issues in the UK. (**T** / **F**)

2. The population of the UK will increase because more babies will be born. (**T** / **F**)

3. Leavers deliberately misled the public about free movement in the EU. (**T** / **F**)

Writing Questions

Make a full sentence, using the following words.

1. The immigration issue (the human rights / focus / of immigrants / on / should).

   _____

2. Many (against / Britain / are / coming to / immigrants / people), because they imagine that immigrants are dangerous.

   _____

Sissinghurst, Cranbrook TN17, UK © glenntonic

Chapter 2

English Gardens

英国式庭園

英国人は庭が好きだ。公開されている庭園を訪れるのは彼らの趣味とも言える。そこでは庭園だけでなく、大きなマナーハウスの建築も楽しめる。Sissinghurst の庭園はその顕著な例だ。また、個人の庭は小さいが、人々は花や植物を植えたり野菜を育てたりして園芸を楽しむ。

Reading 1 ▶ Warm-up

Using your dictionary, find the meanings of the following words.

1. lovingly
2. merge
3. diplomat
4. comprise
5. worth
6. prosperous
7. tranquility
8. culinary

Choose the best answer (a-c).

1. How are public gardens different from private gardens?
   a. Only special people can go into them.
   b. Usually nobody can enter them.
   c. Ordinary people can visit them.

2. What is the main use of special plants?
   a. The use of plants is limited to their beauty.
   b. Plants can be used for medicine.
   c. Providing colour is the main use of all plants.

1 One of the pleasures of visiting or living in England is to visit the many large gardens that are open to the public. These are different from public parks in that they have been lovingly cared for over many years, sometimes centuries, by owners of the large stately homes or castles to which they are attached. They also often cover huge areas of land and ⁵ merge into the countryside that surrounds them. One such is Sissinghurst Castle Garden.

2 Sissinghurst Castle Garden, at Sissinghurst in the Weald of Kent in England, was created in the early 1930s by Vita Sackville-West, poet and writer, and her husband Harold Nicolson, author and diplomat. The ¹⁰ garden comprises a series of ten "rooms", and was one of the earliest examples of this gardening style. Known for its beauty and diversity, the garden at Sissinghurst is among the most famous gardens in England and is well worth a visit.

3 A very different type of garden is the Chelsea Physic Garden, which ¹⁵ is located in a prosperous area of London. This beautiful botanical garden provides peace and tranquility. It was founded by the Worshipful Society of Apothecaries in 1673, the second oldest of its kind in England.

4 In its three and a half acres, there is one of the oldest rock gardens in Europe, a herb garden with culinary and medicinal plants, glasshouses, ²⁰ and rare plants, as well as the largest outdoor olive tree in Britain. A Garden of World Medicine has been added containing plants that are used for medicinal purposes by tribal societies.

NOTES   l. 12: **diversity** 種類の多さ   l. 16: **botanical** 植物の   l. 18: **apothecary** 薬剤師   l. 20: **medicinal**
薬効のある、医薬の   l. 23: **tribal** 種族の、部族の

Comprehension Questions

1. What is the special enjoyment you can get from public gardens?
   a. They are smaller than local public parks.
   b. They are larger and more varied than public parks.
   c. They haven't been looked after by professional gardeners.

2. Sissinghurst Castle Garden was created by...
   a. two poets.
   b. two diplomats.
   c. two writers.

3. When was the garden created?
   a. Less than a hundred years ago
   b. In the 19th century
   c. Just after World War II

4. What does the word 'room' mean here?
   a. A place inside a house
   b. A section of garden with a theme
   c. A place in a garden for storage

5. What is the garden famous for?
   a. Its beauty and its diplomatic owners
   b. Its beauty and its small number of special plants
   c. Its beauty and its wide variety of plants

6. What is unusual about the Chelsea Physic Garden?
   a. It is in the middle of a big city.
   b. It is the oldest garden in the country.
   c. It only has medicinal plants.

7. What is special about this garden?
   a. It has many plants that can be seen in other gardens.
   b. It was created for the purpose of medical research.
   c. It has the largest indoor olive tree in the world.

T/F Questions

Circle T or F for each of the following statements.

1. All gardens in England are open to the public. (**T** / **F**)

2. There were lots of gardens like Sissinghurst before it started. (**T** / **F**)

3. Chelsea Physic Garden contains medicinal plants which are used by primitive tribes. (**T** / **F**)

Writing Questions

Make a full sentence, using the following words.

1. Owners of stately homes take (and / gardens / put / pride / a lot of / in their / effort) into them.

   _____

2. There are botanic gardens (where / in cities / of being with / plants / the calm feeling / you can enjoy)

   _____

A Thatched Cottage © James House

A Private garden © James House

Chapter 2 : English Gardens

Listening

Listen to the following 'Reading 2'. Fill in the correct phrase in each blank (a-e) and match the definitions below.

a. _____ b. _____ c. _____

d. _____ e. _____

1. make something less

2. roughly

3. something that happens that affects something else

4. travel to one's workplace and back home

5. movement in popularity

6. in addition to

7. big change in society

Reading 2 Private Gardens

1 An ordinary garden in the UK is **(a)** 50 feet long and 20 feet wide. It contains 10 different varieties of plants and flowers and usually has a tree. The garden shed is useful for storage and as a hobby room.

2 Gardens began to develop for ordinary people when the cities and
5 towns of England grew **(b)** of the Industrial Revolution. Small town gardens existed before then but they were for the rich. After World War II there was a lot of re-building and the suburbs began to spread and new travel networks made it possible to **(c)**. This trend allowed working people to spend time at the weekends in their gardens planting flowers
10 and shrubs or vegetables.

3 But what are the benefits of gardening? Well, by growing your own garden, you are the one to decide what goes on your plants and into your soil, allowing you to **(d)** of harmful chemicals. Organically growing your own food is sustainable and nourishes your soil by using safe and
15 natural fertilizers and products.

4 There are numerous health benefits too. Gardening is a way of relieving stress and increasing self-esteem. After working in the garden we feel we have achieved something. It also improves heart health and reduces the risk of strokes. It improves hand strength and dexterity (e) improving brain health and reducing the risk of Alzheimer's. Not only 20 that, gardening also relieves depression and improves mental health. A garden with growing plants, is more than "a nice view".

NOTES   l. 1: **feet** foot の複数形   l. 7: **the suburbs** 郊外   l. 10: **shrub** 低木   l. 17: **relieve**〔不安・心配・困難・苦痛などを〕軽減する   l. 17: **self-esteem** 自尊心   l. 19: **dexterity** 器用さ

Comprehension Questions

Choose the best answer (a-c).

1. What is the usual shape of an ordinary garden in the UK?
    a. It is short and wide.
    b. It is long and wide.
    c. It is long and narrow.

2. What is the garden shed for?
    a. It provides a room for visitors.
    b. It is a place for keeping pets.
    c. It is a space for putting things away.

3. How did ordinary gardens develop in the UK?
    a. Towns grew during the 19th century and house gardens were needed.
    b. As the Industrial Revolution grew there was no space left.
    c. Agriculture became less important and people didn't grow plants.

4. Were there private gardens in the towns before the 19th century?
    a. Yes, but they were luxuries for people with money.
    b. Yes, but they were not well looked after.
    c. Yes, but they were too large for people to enjoy.

5. What happened after World War II?
    a. Damaged buildings had to be repaired and this gave space for gardens.
    b. Better transportation allowed people to live further from the town centres.
    c. People didn't have much work after the war and so they spent time on their gardens.

6. What are the good things about having a garden?

    a. You can make money from selling the plants grown in your garden.

    b. You can feed your family on organically grown food from the supermarket.

    c. You can decide on what to plant and how the plants are grown.

7. What are other benefits from gardening?

    a. You can have fun playing in the garden.

    b. You can improve your general health by working in the garden.

    c. You can enjoy the view of other people's gardens.

T/F Questions

Circle T or F for each of the following statements.

1. It's difficult to find sheds in a private garden. (**T** / **F**)

2. People had time to spend on gardens after the Second World War. (**T** / **F**)

3. The benefits of gardening are physical and not mental. (**T** / **F**)

Writing Questions

Make a full sentence, using the following words.

1. Ordinary people started to (years ago / have their / from about / own gardens / 150).

_____

2. Gardening (in a / to people / to be / variety / has proved / of benefit) of ways.

_____

© Nataliia Zhekova / Shutterstock.com
London, United Kingdom–August 24, 2017: British royal family in
Madame Tussauds wax museum in London

Chapter 3

The British Royal Family

英国王室

> 英国王室は日本の皇室と同様、国のシンボルである。英国は共和制だったこともあり、王を処刑した歴史を持つ。よって王室を嫌い、廃止を唱える英国人もいる。在職中のエリザベス 2 世は国民感情を王室につなぎ留めるのにかなり成功しているが、王室の家族をめぐる問題は多い。

Reading 1 ▶ **Warm-up**

Using your dictionary, find the meanings of the following words.

1. monarch
2. commander-in-chief
3. convention
4. parliament
5. majority
6. appoint
7. dismiss
8. prerogative

Choose the best answer (a-c).

1. What does the word 'monarch' mean?
   a. It refers to the head of the family.
   b. It describes the person who is the symbol of the nation.
   c. It is the word that is used for the king of the jungle.

2. What is a constitution?
   a. It is a set of rules for how a country should be governed.
   b. It is a description of the body and how it functions.
   c. It is a law that everyone in the world must follow.

🔊 Audio 06

1 The current monarch of Britain and head of state is Queen Elizabeth II who was crowned in 1953. Her image signifies British sovereignty and appears on stamps, the currency and in public buildings.

2 The royal family carries out various official duties including giving honours, and going on official visits around the country and sometimes abroad. The monarch is the commander-in-chief of the British Armed Forces, but actually her powers are limited by parliament and by convention.

3 Britain is a constitutional monarchy in which the business of government is carried out by the elected members of parliament (MPs). The party with the largest number of MPs forms the government, which has the power to make and pass laws, using its majority of MPs. The judiciary or the law courts are independent of the government and monarch. The Church of England is still the official religion in Britain and the monarch is its head.

4 The monarch must appoint as the prime minister (PM) the head of the party that is the strongest in parliament. She has no choice. She could in theory dismiss the PM but in effect this only happens in electoral defeat, death or resignation.

5 The monarch has rights that are called the royal prerogative, but they cannot be exercised without the advice of the PM. However, she does have the right to be consulted, to encourage, and to warn.

6 According to a recent poll on the royal family the Queen is the most popular at 74% with Prince William third top at 65%. Prince Charles is 6th at 47%.

NOTES l. 2: **crown** 〜を王にする l. 2: **sovereignty** 主権、統治権、支配権 l. 13: **judiciary** 司法（制度）

Comprehension Questions

Choose the best answer (a-c).

1. Queen Elizabeth has reigned for...
   a. just under 65 years.
   b. less than 75 years.
   c. no more than 6 decades.

2. What work does the monarch do?
   a. She gives orders to the military.
   b. She is a travel adviser.
   c. She gives honours to people.

3. A constitutional monarch...
   a. has wide powers to do what she wants.
   b. cannot do much without the permission of parliament.
   c. is not allowed to have any opinions.

4. Under the British Constitution...
   a. the law courts are controlled by parliament.
   b. the law courts listen to the advice of the monarch.
   c. the law courts are free to come to their own decisions.

5. The monarch has no choice but to...
   a. appoint the strongest politician in parliament as PM.
   b. give the job of PM to the head of the biggest party in parliament.
   c. award the position of PM to the politician chosen by the people.

6. The royal prerogative allows the monarch...
   a. certain limited rights over the PM.
   b. to fire the PM as she wishes.
   c. to ignore the advice of the PM.

7. A recent poll on the royal family shows that...
   a. the Queen is the most popular of all.
   b. Charles is more popular than William.
   c. Prince William is as popular as the Queen.

T/F Questions

Circle T or F for each of the following statements.

1. The British Monarch has the right to do a number of things but mostly gives advice. (**T** / **F**)

2. The Prime Minister is the only person who has the power to dismiss the monarch. (**T** / **F**)

3. The political party that has the greatest number of members of parliament forms the government. (**T** / **F**)

Writing Questions

Make a full sentence, using the following words.

1. The British monarchy (over a thousand / despite / in society / has survived / of history / years / great changes).

   _____

2. The royal family carries out (ceremonies, / foreign countries / many duties / visiting / such as / conferring honours, and / attending).

   _____

© mark reinstein / Shutterstock.com
Diana, Princess of Wales leaves the Brazilian Ambassador's residence enroute to the White House.
Washington DC., September 24, 1996.

Listen to the following 'Reading 2'. Fill in the correct phrase in each blank (a-e) and match the definitions below.

a. ▨▨▨▨▨▨▨▨▨ b. ▨▨▨▨▨▨▨▨▨ c. ▨▨▨▨▨▨▨▨▨

d. ▨▨▨▨▨▨▨▨▨ e. ▨▨▨▨▨▨▨▨▨

1. official intention to marry
2. made people like someone
3. badly paid work
4. made differently
5. to be hurt by something
6. not as long as it could be
7. something that did not have a good result

Reading 2 ▸ Princess Diana – Her legacy

1 Diana, Princess of Wales (1961-1997) was the first wife of Charles, Prince of Wales and mother of Princes William and Harry. She was born into nobility as the youngest daughter of the 8th Earl Spencer. She **(a)** by the divorce of her parents.

2 After school she moved to London doing low paying jobs and in 1981   5 **(b)** Prince Charles. They married soon after. It was a fairytale romance and the public fell in love with the princess. But despite the birth of their two sons the marriage failed due to incompatibility and extra-marital affairs. They separated in 1992 and divorced four years later.

3 Diana was celebrated in the media for her support for unconventional 10 charities, particularly AIDS patients, the removal of landmines, and those **(c)** cancer and mental illness.

4 She was highly photogenic and was a leader of fashion in the 80's and 90's. Basically, she was shy but she was also friendly and warm, which **(d)** the public, even after the divorce.   15

5 She died in a car crash, with Dodi Fayed her boyfriend, in a tunnel in Paris, pursued by paparazzi. There was great media and public attention surrounding her death and her funeral was watched by millions on television.

20 **6** What was Diana's legacy? She wanted to be the "People's Princess," but her life was tragically (e). So, did she get the royal family to modernize or did she endanger its future? Will her legacy be her sons? William will one day become the king, but Harry has walked out on the royal family. It's a mixed bag.

NOTES　　l. 3: **nobility** 貴族階級　l. 8: **incompatibility** 性格の不一致　ll. 8-9: **extramarital** 婚外の、不倫の　l. 10: **unconventional** 型破りな、慣例［因習］にとらわれない　l. 11: **landmine** 地雷　l. 17: **paparazzi**（= paparazzo の複数形）〈伊〉パパラッチ、有名人を追いかけるカメラマン

Comprehension Questions

Choose the best answer (a-c).

1. Princess Diana...
    a. had come from an aristocratic family.
    b. was a commoner born into a normal family.
    c. had been divorced before she married Charles.

2. When Diana and Charles married, ...
    a. many people thought it was an unhappy match.
    b. a lot of people felt that they married too quickly.
    c. most people were of the opinion that it was a good thing.

3. Why did Diana attract media attention for her charitable activities?
    a. Because she supported charities that the royal family thought were deserving.
    b. Because she supported charities that did not support the royal family.
    c. Because she supported charities that the royal family traditionally did not.

4. The reason that Diana was loved by the public was because...
    a. she was an attractive and famous fashion model.
    b. she was good-looking and enjoyed the attention of the media.
    c. she looked good on camera and clearly cared for other people.

5. After her divorce from Charles...
    a. many people felt that she was not to blame.
    b. the majority of the public could not forgive her.
    c. most people felt sorry for Prince Charles and not her.

6. Diana's death and funeral...

   a. were followed by huge numbers of people on the media.

   b. were soon forgotten by the people and media.

   c. were the concern of close family and friends only.

7. Princess Diana's legacy has...

   a. damaged the public image of the royal family.

   b. made the royal family more unpopular than before.

   c. changed the royal family in some ways.

T/F Questions

Circle T or F for each of the following statements.

1. The close attention of the media was always something Princess Diana enjoyed. (T / F)

2. The marital problems of Charles and Diana and their subsequent divorce attracted huge attention from the public. (T / F)

3. Diana died peacefully at home surrounded by her family and friends. (T / F)

Writing Questions

Make a full sentence, using the following words.

1. Diana (committed to / causes / in the UK / was / a number of / and the world / social).

   _____

2. She wanted to be remembered (as / as / a member of / royal family / the traditional / rather than / the 'People's Princess').

   _____

Chapter 4

Education in the UK

英国の教育

> 英国人は自国の教育制度を誇りに思っている。子供の可能性を最大限引き出してくれると考えているからだ。しかし、この教育制度には私立学校と公立学校とで差が出ている。ブレグジットや未曾有の事態に直面した昨今、高等教育を含む教育制度は新しい問題に向き合わねばならない。

Reading 1 ▶ ## Warm-up

Using your dictionary, find the meanings of the following words.

1. legally   2. categorise   3. undertake   4. assessment

5. sufficiently   6. qualify   7. require   8. grade

Choose the best answer (a-c).

1. This text is about...

   a. how to get into the British education system.

   b. how to pass English exams in the system.

   c. how the education system operates in the UK.

2. Which university is the oldest in the UK?

   a. Edinburgh

   b. Oxford

   c. London

Reading 1 — The Education System

🔊 Audio 08

1 The education system in the UK is divided into four main parts; primary education, secondary education, further education and higher education. Children in the UK are legally required to attend school from about 5 years of age until they are 16.

2 Primary and secondary education is categorised into Key Stages, as follows

    Key Stage 1: 5 to 7 years old

    Key Stage 2: 7 to 11 years old

    Key Stage 3: 11 to 14 years old

    Key Stage 4: 14 to 16 years old

Generally, Key Stages 1 and 2 are undertaken at primary school and at 11 years old a student moves on to secondary school and completes Key Stages 3 and 4.

3 Students must pass national tests at the end of each stage. The most important assessment occurs at age 16 when students take their GCSEs or General Certificate of Secondary Education. This normally consists of around six subjects. This system applies to England and Wales, but Scotland and Northern Ireland have slightly different systems of education.

4 Once students complete their GCSEs, they can finish school and go into the world of work. Or, if they pass their GCSEs sufficiently well, they can choose to go on to take A-levels for university entrance or the BTEC, which qualifies students for certain careers. However, because of the pandemic some of these exams will be replaced by assessments or postponed. Most universities require a minimum of three subjects to apply for entrance, and each university has its own grade requirements. In addition to A-levels, some universities such as Oxford and Cambridge (known as Oxbridge) have entrance exams and interviews as well.

NOTES   l. 17: **subject**〔教育の〕科目、教科 l. 23: **BTEC**=Business and Technology Education Council《英》
商業技術教育委員会

Comprehension Questions

Choose the best answer (a-c).

1. Until what age is going to school compulsory?
   a. Five years of age
   b. Sixteen years of age
   c. Eighteen years of age

2. What is the purpose of the Key Stages?
   a. To divide up the years of education for the benefit of administrators
   b. To check on the progress of students regularly
   c. To make it hard for students to complete their education

3. What happens at eleven years of age?
   a. Pupils pass from primary to secondary education.
   b. Pupils have the option to leave school.
   c. Pupils leave secondary and go into further education.

4. Why is the age of 16 so important?
   a. Because pupils have to go to university.
   b. Because pupils must leave school and face the world of work.
   c. Because students need to decide if they wish to study further.

5. What is the difference between GCSEs and A-levels?
   a. The difference is the number of subjects that can be taken.
   b. The A-level courses are of a higher level.
   c. GCSEs are sufficient qualifications to allow entry to universities.

6. What does the BTEC qualification prepare students for?
   a. It is a non-academic course to qualify students for a career.
   b. It is a technical qualification designed to help students work with their hands.
   c. It is for students who wish to start work at 16.

7. How do students move from one Key Stage to the next?
   a. They have to pass national tests.
   b. They are recommended by their class teachers.
   c. They automatically move from one stage to another.

T/F Questions

Circle T or F for each of the following statements.

1. Britain's education system consists of four main divisions. (**T** / **F**)

2. All universities in Britain require candidates to take an entrance test. (**T** / **F**)

3. Students are limited to taking three subjects at A-level. (**T** / **F**)

Writing Questions

Make a full sentence, using the following words.

1. Getting into Oxford or Cambridge (have to / at A-level / because / is difficult / do / applicants / very well) and also undergo entrance tests.

   _____

2. The primary and secondary education system (the progress / at every / is designed / of students / Key Stage / to check on) in their education to make sure targets are achieved.

   _____

Listen to the following 'Reading 2'. Fill in the correct phrase in each blank (a-e) and match the definitions below.

a. ░░░░░░░░░░░░░░░░ b. ░░░░░░░░░░░░░░░░ c. ░░░░░░░░░░░░░░░░

d. ░░░░░░░░░░░░░░░░ e. ░░░░░░░░░░░░░░░░

1. the work of scholars that appears in print
2. society based on free-lance work
3. opportunities for university students to study or work abroad
4. cover a number of categories
5. discouraged from taking part
6. an educational institution that teaches through TV and radio
7. to be connected from one to another

UNIVERSITY OF OXFORD

Reading 2 ▸ Issues for the Universities

1 Britain has over 130 universities, **(a)** 13th century Oxbridge to 19th century London and 20th century Sheffield, not forgetting newer ones like the **(b)** (1969) which teaches mainly through TV and radio. How are they going to fare in the coming years?

5 **2** Universities are in a challenging global market, partly because Brexit is making many potential European students stay away. Also, the present flow of British students who go to study in Europe, notably on the renowned Erasmus program, could be endangered.

3 Attracting and retaining high-level academic staff from Europe may
10 become increasingly difficult. In 2014, 28% of 194,000 academics were non-UK nationals, 16% from the EU.

4 Also, sustaining research and creating innovation within Britain will be difficult. Recent figures show that 70% of UK researchers **(c)** outside the UK.

15 **5** Universities also face increasing costs and less revenue as pension costs spiral and government money for research is cut. Raising fees is difficult as students face mounting debts. The International University

Lifestyle Survey 2017 found that 60% of students are avoiding socializing to save money. This leads to loneliness that (d) problems in academic performance and mental health.

6 Also, developing students' skills is a challenge and universities need to work with companies to create more apprenticeships and placements to achieve this. And more online degree courses that are cheap and flexible are needed. Partnerships with alternative providers such as Facebook are a possibility, offering services to (e) worker who needs to continually re-train.

7 Universities must balance heritage and knowledge with the need to be agile players in a changing world.

NOTES   l. 7: **present flow** 現在の流れ   l. 12: **sustain** 〔努力などを〕持続させる   l. 15: **pension** 年金   l. 16: **spiral** 急上昇する   l. 22: **apprenticeship** 見習い（期間）、実習   l. 26: **re-train** ～を再教育をする   l. 28: **agile** 〔動作が〕機敏な

Comprehension Questions

Choose the best answer (a-c).

1. London University...
   a. is one of the oldest in the UK.
   b. was founded decades ago.
   c. has a history of more than 150 years.

2. The Open University...
   a. provides courses on a traditional campus.
   b. offers courses that are easier than other universities.
   c. gives many of its classes through the media.

3. Because of Brexit...
   a. UK universities will have difficulties collecting EU students.
   b. British students will not be able to study abroad.
   c. EU students will be able to study in the UK for free.

4. A recent survey shows that British universities...
   a. have a large percentage of foreign academics.
   b. do not encourage foreign teachers to join them.
   c. need to send more academics to the EU.

5. Most British academics...

   a. have their research published in the UK.

   b. do not publish in the UK.

   c. publish their research in foreign countries.

6. The reasons for the universities' financial problems include...

   a. the high salaries of the professors.

   b. the fact that the government is not giving any money to them.

   c. the cost of the pensions for former employees.

7. Recently students are...

   a. spending too much money on having fun instead of studying.

   b. unable to have fun with their friends because they lack money.

   c. more interested in saving their money for investment.

T/F Questions

Circle T or F for each of the following statements.

1. Universities need to reform their current model of educating students. (**T** / **F**)

2. Gig economy workers have guaranteed lifetime employment. (**T** / **F**)

3. Universities have to link up with companies to prepare students for the world of work. (**T** / **F**)

Writing Questions

Make a full sentence, using the following words.

1. Over the coming years British universities will face many challenges and although (may face / some / new eventualities, / ride / are prepared for / others / a bumpy).

   _____

2. Some university students are suffering because (enough money / and this / mental stress / don't have / can lead to / to live on / they) and lowered academic performance.

   _____

Chapter 5

Eating in Britain

英国の食事事情

English breakfast (top) and sausage rolls (bottom)

> 昔から英国の料理はまずいと言われてきた。そんな料理に変化が見えつつある。家庭では TV やインターネットの料理番組が人気だ。レストランでは上品な料理が提供されるようになっている。しかし、本通りで目につくのは相変わらずファーストフードに群がる人々だ。

Reading 1 ▶ ## Warm-up

Using your dictionary, find the meanings of the following words.

1. wrapped 　　 2. comprising 　　 3. brunch 　　 4. minced

5. dishes 　　 6. traditional 　　 7. dominate 　　 8. afford

Choose the best answer (a-c).

1. What kind of food do many British people enjoy most?
   - **a.** Raw fish
   - **b.** Pies and pasties
   - **c.** Fine French food

2. The word 'typical' means...
   - **a.** dramatic.
   - **b.** famous.
   - **c.** usual.

Typical British Dining

🔊 Audio 10

1 Perhaps the most iconic British dish is fish and chips: deep fried cod or plaice with fried potatoes and mushy peas. As a takeout it is wrapped in paper and sprinkled with salt and malt vinegar.

2 Other favorites include the Sunday roast comprising different roasted meats such as chicken breast, turkey, pork or beef served with seasonal vegetables, roast potatoes and lashings of gravy.

3 The English breakfast is not usually eaten every day as it might damage your health. Usually it is eaten at the weekend as brunch. It consists of fried or poached egg, fried bacon, sausage, and often tomatoes or mushrooms. Fried bread is sometimes added as are hash browns.

4 The British are fond of all kinds of pies and pasties, such as shepherd's pie, made of minced lamb, and fish pie. Cornish pasties are made of pastry filled with minced beef and vegetables. Also pork pies and sausage rolls are popular. Toad in the hole, bangers and mash, and pigs in a blanket are all dishes that include sausages and have funny names.

Toad in the hole

5 British cooking is also famous for its desserts, or puddings as the British call them. Traditional trifle is a favorite and often includes strawberries. It is made of cake rolls, custard, jelly and cream. It is very sweet and gives you a sugar rush.

6 The cream tea was originally created for the upper classes as a snack between lunch and dinner. A favorite with foreign visitors, it consists of scones with clotted cream and jam, washed down with a nice cup of tea.

7 Although fast food dominates high streets, fine dining does exist for those who can afford it, which is usually French cuisine. Indian, Chinese and Italian takeaways are common. Changes in drinking habits mean that many local pubs have become family restaurants.

NOTES　　　l. 1: **cod** タラ◆ Atlantic cod、Pacific cod 等を指す　l. 2: **plaice** （ヨーロッパ・）プレイス◆ヨーロッパ産のカレイ科ツノガレイ属の食用魚　l. 2: **pea** エンドウ豆　l. 3: **sprinkle with** ～を振りかける　l. 3: **malt** モルト、麦芽、麦もやし◆麦の種子を発芽させたもの　l. 6: **lashings of** 〈主に英・話〉たくさんの、多量の　l. 10: **hash browns** ハッシュ（ト）・ブラウン、ハッシュトポテト◆ゆでたジャガイモを焼いたり揚げたりしたもの　l. 26: **clotted cream** 〈英〉クロテッド・クリーム◆乳脂肪分が55％～60％の濃厚なクリーム　l. 26: **wash ~ down with ...** ～を…で（胃の中に）流し込む　l. 29: **takeaway** 〈英〉持ち帰り用の料理

Comprehension Questions

Choose the best answer (a-c).

1. How is 'fish and chips' described in this text?
   a. It is one of the most famous British dishes.
   b. The way it is cooked is described in detail.
   c. It is a dish eaten in restaurants, not a takeaway.

2. What is the main ingredient of the Sunday roast?
   a. Roasted vegetables
   b. Roasted potatoes
   c. Roasted meat

3. Why could eating too many English breakfasts harm your health?
   a. Because nearly every item in the meal is fried.
   b. Because there are no vegetables in the dish.
   c. Because it is too much food to eat at lunchtime.

4. Why is one of the dishes called 'shepherd's pie'?
   a. Because it is only eaten by people who look after sheep.
   b. Because it contains the meat of young sheep.
   c. Because the topping is made of potato rather than pastry.

5. Choose the best description of 'trifle' below.
   a. It is a fruit pie that is covered in cream.
   b. It is a pudding made of pastry and a custard topping.
   c. It is a sweet mix of custard, jelly, fruit and cream.

6. The Cream Tea...
   a. was created for upper class foreign visitors.
   b. was originally meant to be eaten in the afternoon.
   c. is a kind of English tea taken with cream.

7. Although fast food is popular in Britain, ...
   a. most people can afford fine dining.
   b. Indian, Chinese and Italian cooking are favored by many.
   c. the British prefer to go to pubs and just drink.

T/F Questions

Circle T or F for each of the following statements.

1. Takeout fish and chips are covered with ketchup to improve the taste. (**T** / **F**)

2. British people are fond of every type of pie. (**T** / **F**)

3. Nowadays, fast food is widely popular with British consumers. (**T** / **F**)

Writing Questions

Make a full sentence, using the following words.

1. (a / and / sweet / people / tooth / have / British) therefore enjoy eating desserts and puddings.

   _____

2. Only those (can / restaurants / are / go to / fine dining / who / well off) regularly.

   _____

Trifle

Shepherd's pie

British Traditional fish and chips

Sunday roast

Listen to the following 'Reading 2'. Fill in the correct phrase in each blank (a-e) and match the definitions below.

a. ▨▨▨▨▨▨▨▨▨ b. ▨▨▨▨▨▨▨▨ c. ▨▨▨▨▨▨▨▨

d. ▨▨▨▨▨▨▨▨ e. ▨▨▨▨▨▨▨

1. on the other hand

2. in spite of everything

3. good food for the body

4. getting fat

5. places not in the centres of cities

6. places where the rich live

7. result in

Reading 2 — Poor Diet

1 "A diet of potatoes and weak tea unavoidably engenders a multitude of diseases." So said the Victorian social scientist, Friedrich Engels in *The Condition of the Working Class in England* in 1845.

2 What has changed since? Well, **(a)** the advice of TV chefs, cookery books and healthy-eating plans many British people still eat poorly. The problem is that, often, healthy food costs more than unhealthy food. The cheapest and quickest way to get a hundred calories of food energy into your body is through sugars, fats and processed starches.

3 Some years ago a study in obesity checked the cost of getting one hundred calories from various types of food. One hundred calories-worth of broccoli cost 51p, **(b)** one hundred calories of frozen chips cost 2p. Nutritious food such as fruits, fresh vegetables, lean meats, fish, and grains – are, for many, too expensive.

4 Big supermarkets that offer a wide variety of quality foods at fair prices are usually found in wealthier suburbs and **(c)** for car-owning customers. In deprived areas the poor tend to shop at convenience and corner stores where food can cost up to 13% more for a nutritionally adequate diet.

5 Poor diet can (d) obesity, anaemia,
20 diabetes, raised blood pressure, heart
and vascular disease, strokes and
cancers of the stomach and oesophagus.

6 In Victorian times, most people
could only afford to eat bread and
25 potatoes and starvation was not rare.
However, the modern British poor
although unlikely to suffer from
starvation are more likely to fall ill from eating a diet lacking in (e).

© 1000 Words
London, UK: Citrus fruit is seen in an aisle of a Tesco supermarket.

NOTES   l. 1: **weak** 薄い、（ここでは）出がらしの   l. 1: **engender** 〜を生じさせる   ll. 1-2: **a multitude of:**
多くの   l. 8: **starch** (小麦) でんぷん   l. 16: **deprived** 貧しい   l. 18: **adequate** 適切な、十分な   l. 19: **anaemia** 〈英〉
貧血   l. 21: **vascular** 脈管の、血管の   l. 22: **oesophagus** 食道

Comprehension Questions

Choose the best answer (a-c).

1. What was Engels writing about in his book?
   a. The history of the British upper class
   b. The medical condition of the people of Britain
   c. The situation of ordinary people in Britain

2. How have matters changed in the UK?
   a. The poor people of Britain are eating more nutritional food.
   b. British people are eating too much processed food.
   c. Ordinary British people know more about eating healthily.

3. What is the main problem that makes it difficult for people to eat healthily?
   a. People cannot afford to eat good food.
   b. People find it easier to eat fast food.
   c. People want to get food energy calories into their bodies quickly.

4. What was the study originally about?
   a. The cost of living
   b. The price of broccoli as compared to fried potatoes
   c. People who are overweight

5. Why is it difficult for the poor to purchase quality food?

   a. Because they live in places where there are few good supermarkets.

   b. Because they prefer to go to convenience stores to shop.

   c. Because they don't want to drive to out-of-town sites to do their shopping.

6. What would probably happen if you ate poor quality food over a long period of time?

   a. You would feel hungry all the time and eat more than you should.

   b. Your taste buds would be damaged and you would not be able to appreciate good food.

   c. Your health would suffer and you would probably get seriously ill.

7. What is happening with the British poor now?

   a. They are eating a diet of unhealthy food.

   b. They are eating too much bread and too many potatoes.

   c. They often don't get enough to eat and starve.

T/F Questions

Circle T or F for each of the following statements.

1. Because there is a lot of information about eating a healthy diet, most British people eat well. (**T** / **F**)

2. Many poor people do not have access to reasonably priced good food. (**T** / **F**)

3. Engels believed that potatoes and weak tea were enough to provide a balanced diet. (**T** / **F**)

Writing Questions

Make a full sentence, using the following words.

1. Fredrich Engels was a (social / who / British poor / famous / wrote / scientist / about the).

   _____

2. The low quality diet of many poorer people in the UK (health problems / obesity / and / often leads to / other).

   _____

© AlanMorris / Shutterstock.com

Chapter 6

Health and the Medical System

健康と医療システム

> 英国人にとって NHS はとても大切な制度である。戦後、労働政権が設立し、国民の誰もが無料で治療を受けられるようになった。それ以後、家庭医と病院、そして老人ホームが国民の健康を支えてきた。コロナウイルスの大流行で国民は NHS の価値を再認識することとなっている。

Reading 1 ▶ ## Warm-up

Using your dictionary, find the meanings of the following words.

1. principle
2. stuff (v)
3. inception
4. dog (v)
5. committee
6. efficient
7. markedly
8. plummet (v)

Choose the best answer (a-c).

1. This article is about...
   a. private medicine in the UK.
   b. getting medical insurance from a UK company.
   c. how the British medical system works.

2. The letters NHS stand for...
   a. the National Health Service.
   b. the National Healthy System.
   c. the Natural Health Service.

The National Health Service (NHS)

1 After World War II in 1945 a new Labour government was elected and promised a revolution in health care. The health minister was Aneurin Bevan. He wanted a health service based on four principles: free at the point of use, available to everyone in need, paid for out of general taxation, and used responsibly. Faced with the threat of a strike 5 by doctors, he offered them more money and allowed them to do private work on the side. As he famously said, "I stuffed their mouths with gold".

2 In 1948 the first person was treated on the NHS and the system has been looking after the nation's health since. But the problem of money 10 has dogged the service since it was founded and in 1951 prescription charges for outpatients' drugs were introduced, but still subsidized by the government. Since then demands of medical science have continued to push up costs. When the Conservative Party re-gained power, they formed a committee of experts to look at how health care costs could be 15 reduced. The committee reported that the NHS was efficient, cost-effective and deserved more money. The Conservative government had to accept the results.

3 The NHS has proved its value ever since; life expectancy has markedly increased, infant mortality has plummeted, vaccinations have 20 increased, smoking has dramatically decreased (from 65% for men in 1948 to 25% today) and around 50,000 people are treated in the Accident and Emergency wards each day. One of the biggest employers in Europe, the NHS remains more cost-effective than the American private health system. 25

NOTES l. 1: **Labour government** 労働党政権 l. 4: **pay for out of ~** ~から支払う l. 7: **on the side** 副業で l. 11: **prescription** 処方箋 l. 12: **subsidize** 〔政府が私企業や団体に〕助成金を払う l. 15: **look at** ~を検討する l. 17: **deserve** ~に値する、~の価値がある l. 24: **private** 民間の

Comprehension Questions

Choose the best answer (a-c).

1. After the Second World War...
   a. there was a revolution in Britain.
   b. the Labour government wanted to change everything.
   c. the new government wanted to improve health care.

2. The Health Minister, Mr. Bevan...
   a. proposed a free health service.
   b. wanted people to be responsible for their own health.
   c. said that the country should pay people to be sick.

3. Bevan's four principles included...
   a. private health care for everyone.
   b. free medical provision for government workers only.
   c. paying for medical care from taxes.

4. When doctors said they would go on strike, Bevan...
   a. threatened them with violence.
   b. agreed to pay them more.
   c. let them charge NHS patients for medical care.

5. As a way to control costs the government...
   a. charged outpatients for visits to the doctor.
   b. made inpatients pay for hospital treatment.
   c. required outpatients to pay part of the cost of medicines.

6. The costs of running the NHS increased because of...
   a. the expense of medical research.
   b. the high salaries of doctors.
   c. the ever increasing numbers of patients.

7. When the Conservative government got into power,...
   a. it wanted to find a cheaper way of providing health care.
   b. it did not want to change a system that was working well.
   c. it wrote a report that was critical of the NHS.

T/F Questions

> Circle T or F for each of the following statements.

1. The Conservative government of the time was happy with the NHS and didn't want to change things. (**T** / **F**)

2. By most criteria the NHS has performed well in looking after the health of the nation. (**T** / **F**)

3. The American private health insurance system is much more efficient than the British NHS. (**T** / **F**)

Writing Questions

> Make a full sentence, using the following words.

1. The British health minister of the day, Aneurin Bevan, (system / to the British / proposed / change / medical / a radical).

   _____

2. The British people have (over seventy / benefitted from / in many ways / years ago / began / the NHS / since it).

   _____

Listen to the following 'Reading 2'. Fill in the correct phrase in each blank (a-e) and match the definitions below.

a. _____ b. _____ c. _____

d. _____ e. _____

1. doing one's job in one's house

2. continued to operate as normal

3. looking after people in hospital who are in danger

4. providing goods as they are needed

5. to give extra support

6. to use something for a proposal

7. to beg someone for something

Reading 2 — The Coronavirus Pandemic

1 When the coronavirus reached the UK, the government under Boris Johnson, decided to do things differently from Continental Europe, which was closing schools, enforcing quarantine and putting soldiers on the streets.

5 **2** In the UK pubs, restaurants, theatres and sporting venues **(a)**; only the over-70s and those with flu-like symptoms were advised to stay at home. Top government scientists advised this low-key response **(b)** the theory that if the virus spreads naturally it will build up "herd immunity" in the population.

10 **3** Leading immunologists challenged the soundness of this theory. Their scientific analysis showed the NHS would be overwhelmed and it would lead to around 250,000 deaths.

4 Prime Minister Johnson said "drastic action" was necessary and people should **(c)** and avoid unnecessary travel and social contact. But

15 many scientists say this is not enough. In France, President Macron warned that the country was "in a state of war" and announced mandatory bans on movement **(d)** fines.

5 Fear of an imminent lockdown in the UK has led to widespread panic buying at supermarkets, stripping shelves as retailers (e) shoppers not to stockpile. Britain imports around half its food and the "just-in-time" supply system means there are few warehouses with stocks of food ready for emergency distribution.

6 Ironically, Johnson was diagnosed with COVID-19 and was subsequently hospitalised in intensive care. In this turmoil, Queen Elizabeth recorded a moving and thoughtful speech that was aired on TV and watched by nearly 24 million viewers. Towards the end she said, "We will meet again" and gave the nation hope.

20

25

NOTES　　　l. 3: **quarantine** 検疫　l. 7: **low-key** 〔人の態度などが〕控えめな　l. 8: **herd** 群衆　l. 10: **soundness** 正当性　l. 17: **mandatory** 強制的な　l. 20: **stockpile** 〈話〉買いだめする　l. 23: **diagnose ~ with ...** ～を…と診断する　l. 24: **turmoil** 混乱

Comprehension Questions

Choose the best answer (a-c).

1. At first, the British government's response to the coronavirus…

   a. was different from that of other European countries.

   b. was in line with what was happening in other countries worldwide.

   c. was to ignore it completely and carry on as normal.

2. On the Continent of Europe many governments…

   a. were taking rather soft measures against the virus.

   b. were forcing people to stay in their homes to slow the spread of the virus.

   c. were putting soldiers on the streets to shoot those who had left their homes.

3. The UK government at the beginning…

   a. didn't give any advice to the people concerning the virus.

   b. advised elderly people not to go out.

   c. suggested that only those who had the flu needed to go to hospital.

4. The advice of government scientists was based on the theory that…

   a. the spread of the virus would give people immunity.

   b. since there is no vaccine then a number of people will die anyway.

   c. not many people will get the virus and so normal life should be maintained.

5. Most scientists who specialized in viruses…
   a. supported the government's management of the crisis.
   b. did not agree with the government's belief in "herd immunity".
   c. could not find evidence to dispute the government's view.

6. The scientific data…
   a. showed that the government's approach would lead to too many deaths.
   b. made it clear that the number of deaths from the virus would be acceptable.
   c. was shocking but did not change the government's policies.

7. The measures that the Prime Minister announced after criticism by scientists included:
   a. working from home and ordering food online.
   b. avoiding unnecessary contact and leaving work early.
   c. not travelling unless necessary and keeping away from other people.

T/F Questions

Circle T or F for each of the following statements.

1. In France, the president announced that people would be fined if they did not stand still. (**T** / **F**)

2. People in the UK lost trust in the government and were frightened that life would get much worse. (**T** / **F**)

3. In the Queen's speech she suggested that the COVID-19 pandemic would be overcome. (**T** / **F**)

Writing Questions

Make a full sentence, using the following words.

1. Despite pleas by supermarket executives and staff (by customers / goods / led to / being stripped of / buying / panic / shelves).

   _____

2. The early low-key response to the coronavirus by the British government (to spread / infection / and take / allowed / leading it / course / to change) "drastic action."

   _____

© Kamira / Shutterstock.com
The Beatles Story exhibition in Liverpool

Chapter 7

Music & Fashion

音楽とファッション

> 芸術や創作活動は英国人の生活に不可欠だ。英国生まれの The Beatles は世界で最も有名なロックバンドだろう。ロックの公演活動の多くは彼らが生まれたリバプールで行なわれる。一方、ファッションと言えば、パリ、ミラノ、ニューヨークが中心と思われがちだが、ロンドンも忘れてはならない。

Reading 1 ▶ Warm-up

Using your dictionary, find the meanings of the following words.

1. genre   2. mixture   3. nominate   4. fab
5. boast   6. attend   7. scene   8. vibrant

Choose the best answer (a-c).

1. The Beatles were...
   a. family cars invented in Germany.
   b. a famous pop group.
   c. insects, popular with children.

2. Liverpool is...
   a. a small lake near London.
   b. a football team in Scotland.
   c. a city in the north-west of England.

1 When thinking of music in the UK, the first name that comes to mind is the Beatles and Liverpool was where the members of the group were born. The River Mersey passes through the
5 city and their genre of music, which is a mixture of pop and rock, is called the 'Merseybeat'.

LIVERPOOL: The Cavern Club, the legendary venue where The Beatles popularity started © Kamira

2 Recently, Liverpool was nominated as the *World Capital City of Pop*. The musicians of Liverpool have produced 56 number one hits in
10 the UK, more than any other city in the world. As well as the Fab Four, the city also gave us Gerry and the Pacemakers, and Billy Fury.

3 Not only pop and rock, Liverpool also boasts the Royal Liverpool Philharmonic, Britain's longest surviving orchestra. The Liverpool
15 International Music Festival takes place every summer in Sefton Park. It is Europe's biggest free music event and attracts local talent as well as musicians from far and wide.

4 Africa Oye, a huge musical event held in Liverpool, is the largest festival of African music in the UK. It's free and around 50,000 people
20 attend each time. So, Liverpool is not only about John, Paul, George and Ringo, but also has a lively music scene involving many other musicians and music genres.

5 Outside of Liverpool there are other cities in the UK where you can find a large and vibrant music scene. One such is Manchester where the
25 music scene is so lively that it is known as 'Madchester' by the music media. And of course, London is the magnet for musicians from all over the UK.

NOTES   l. 4: **River Mersey** マージー川◆イングランド北西部を流れる川   l. 21: **lively** 活発な   l. 26: **magnet for ~** ～を引きつけるもの

Comprehension Questions

Choose the best answer (a-c).

1. When we think of pop/rock music, we think of the Beatles because...
   a. they were born in Liverpool.
   b. they became so famous everywhere.
   c. their music was better than any other.

2. Where does the name Merseyside come from?
   a. A big river
   b. A huge hill
   c. A holy church

3. Why has Liverpool been nominated as the *World Capital of Pop*?
   a. Because so many musicians were born there.
   b. Because lots of songs written there became hits.
   c. Because the city has hosted many music festivals.

4. In Liverpool, pop and rock music...
   a. is not the only kind of music performed there.
   b. have limited other genres of music played there.
   c. showed that other types of music were outdated.

5. The Liverpool International Music Festival...
   a. is the largest in the world.
   b. does not welcome local bands.
   c. has no entrance fee.

6. Africa Oye is a musical event that is...
   a. designed to honour the Beatles.
   b. for African people only.
   c. very popular with thousands of visitors.

7. Manchester is called 'Madchester' because...
   a. the music scene there is very lively.
   b. the musicians who play there are crazy.
   c. the music events there get dangerous.

T/F Questions

Circle T or F for each of the following statements.

1. All the members of the Beatles band were born in the Liverpool area. (**T** / **F**)

2. Merseybeat is a word that describes a mixture of classical and rock music. (**T** / **F**)

3. The city of Liverpool has produced many pop groups and more number one hits than any other UK city. (**T** / **F**)

Writing Questions

Make a full sentence, using the following words.

1. One of the biggest bands of all time (the Beatles / still sung / be / whose songs / has to / all over the world / are) many decades after they were first recorded.

_____

2. Manchester is one of the (and it / in the UK / a vibrant / as well / biggest cities / boasts / musical scene).

_____

© Featureflash Photo Agency / Shutterstock.com
Cara Delevingne at London Fashion Week SS14–
Topshop Unique–Catwalk, London.

© Featureflash Photo Agency / Shutterstock.com
Kate Moss at London Fashion Week SS14–Topshop Unique–Arrivals, London.

© Vasilisa Petruk / Shutterstock.com
LONDON–FEBRUARY 15, 2019: London Fashion Week 2019.

Reading 2 **Listening**

🔊 Audio 15

Listen to the following 'Reading 2'. Fill in the correct phrase in each blank (a-e) and match the definitions below.

a. _____ b. _____ c. _____

d. _____ e. _____

1. a place that is the centre
2. connected to
3. not less than
4. from different parts of the world
5. register for
6. has a value of
7. as well as

Reading 2   Fashion in the UK

1 Since **(a)** 1666 when King Charles II resolved to set a fashion for clothes, fashion has been an important part of the way British people define themselves. It is big business too, as the UK's fashion industry **(b)** 26 billion pounds and employs 800,000 people.

2 In addition to the hard economic benefits it gives, fashion also has a 5 soft power side. The UK is a world leader in fashion education. Six of the top twenty fashion universities are based in the UK. These are very international institutions and an estimated 1,500 international students enroll on such courses each year.

3 London Fashion Week is one of the 'big four' international fashion 10 festivals. It is a showcase for the industry and for the many talented people who work in it. Now London is beginning to replace the traditional cities of New York, Paris and Milan **(c)** for new, young and **(d)** fashion designers and artists.

4 In 2014 Ipsos Mori surveyed countries that are particularly important 15 to the UK. It showed that 22% of young people said fashion was something that made the UK attractive to them, while 15% said design was.

5 Famous individuals have (e) certain clothes; from Lord Wellington's
20 boots to Diana's dresses. The wearers often consciously use these marks
of fashion to give an image of themselves or their nation.

6 The world of fashion has a powerful influence on society, politics and
culture, as in the 17th century when Charles II encouraged new fashions
to reduce France's influence on English life.

NOTES　　　l. 1: **resolve**〔〜しようと〕決心する　l. 4: **pound**《貨幣単位》ポンド◆英国の貨幣単位で 100 ペン
スに相当　l. 5: **hard economic benefit**お金と雇用を指す　l. 6: **soft power**文化や教育を指す　l. 11: **showcase**〔長
所を引き出すような〕展示〔紹介〕の場　l. 19: **lord**〈英〉〔称号の〕卿

Comprehension Questions

Choose the best answer (a-c).

1. King Charles II decided to set the fashion because...
   a. he wanted to be a fashion designer.
   b. he wanted to buy expensive foreign clothes but could not afford them.
   c. he wanted England to be a leader of fashion.

2. Fashion is not just about clothes design...
   a. it also takes money out of the economy.
   b. it is also a way to show people how rich you are.
   c. it can also lead to a career in the industry.

3. Soft power includes fashion education...
   a. and Britain is trying to get into this market.
   b. in which Britain is already a leader.
   c. for which Britain is not well prepared now.

4. London Fashion Week...
   a. is a place for people to show others their abilities.
   b. is an event that doesn't attract much interest in the world.
   c. is for models to show off while walking along the runway.

5. Why is London Fashion Week important for the industry?
   a. Because designers want to sell their work there.
   b. Because the buyers want to find bargains among the design products.
   c. Because it is challenging the power of other, older centres of fashion.

6. Recent research shows that...

   a. some young people abroad are interested in the UK because of its fashion environment.

   b. fashion is not a strong reason for young people to come to the UK.

   c. the fashion industry should focus on selling clothes to young people abroad.

7. Well known people often use their fashion sense to...

   a. put forward an image they want others to admire.

   b. show others how much money they have spent.

   c. advertise the clothes they are wearing.

T/F Questions

Circle T or F for each of the following statements.

1. Some of the top schools for fashion education are located in the UK. (**T** / **F**)

2. Fashion is for people to make money and show off but has no impact on the nation. (**T** / **F**)

3. The late Princess Diana was famous as a fashion icon and for the dresses she wore. (**T** / **F**)

Writing Questions

Make a full sentence, using the following words.

1. Fashion is important not only as a way for people to express their individuality (many thousands / as an important / the economy / but also / of people / employing / part of).

   _____

2. (one of the / London / fashion / has / of the world / hubs / become), challenging the traditional centres of Paris, Milan and New York.

   _____

Costa Brava, Spain

Chapter *8*

Tourism

観光事業

> 英国人は休暇を大事にする。夏休みは 2 〜 3 週間と長く、彼らは太陽やビーチを求めてスペインやギリシャに繰り出す。毎晩パーティを楽しみ、羽目を外すこともある。同様に、多くの外国人が英国にやって来る。彼らは息を飲むほど美しい自然や文化との触れ合いを求めている。

Reading 1 ▶ Warm-up

Using your dictionary, find the meanings of the following words.

1. Brits
2. opt to
3. priority
4. return
5. boring
6. bucket list
7. getaway (n)
8. observe

Choose the best answer (a-c).

1. Outbound tourism means...
   a. tourists who leave the country.
   b. tourists who come into the country.
   c. tourists within the country.

2. Expectations and disappointments mean...
   a. something you don't look forward to and something that depresses you.
   b. something you are worried about and something unfortunate.
   c. something you hope for and something you feel unhappy about.

Reading 1 — Outbound Tourism - Expectations & Disappointments

🔊 Audio 16

1 After Christmas comes to an end, over three million Brits opt to book their summer holiday. The firm favourites are Spain and the USA. Recent research found that when it comes to booking holidays, top priorities for consumers include guaranteed sunshine, a nearby beach and even access to British TV programmes. 5

2 But more than half of Britain's sun-seekers have gone on a holiday then wished they had not bothered. A survey of 2,000 adults by a cruise company found 57 per cent return regretting their choice of holiday. This includes those who had been to the same place before.

3 The average Brit has been to the same destination four times. One in 10 four said the excitement of finding new things to do there had worn off even by their second visit. The typical adult goes on three boring holidays over a lifetime. It seems as people get older, they get less satisfied with their holiday, but also less ambitious.

4 This fear of going somewhere new can lead to regret, as up to 40 per 15 cent admit they may never get to see great places on their bucket list such as the Great Wall of China, Mt. Fuji, or the Pyramids. Not going to new places also leads to 'holiday envy' as 40 per cent say they have felt jealous of a friend's getaway, after hearing their glowing reports.

5 COVID-19 has hurt the tourist industry badly and it will take years 20 to recover. Travellers have to observe the "new normal" rules or face a heavy fine.

NOTES   l. 1: **come to an end** 終わる   l. 1: **book** 〜の予約をする   ll. 21-22: **face a fine** 罰金を科される

Comprehension Questions

Choose the best answer (a-c).

1. Usually British people book their summer holidays...
   a. shortly before they go.
   b. a year in advance.
   c. about 6 months before leaving.

2. What do British people want when they go on holiday?
   a. Lots of sun and beaches close by
   b. Sunny weather and good local TV programmes
   c. Sandy beaches and local food

3. How do many British tourists feel about their holiday?
   a. They wish they could have had a longer stay.
   b. They are unhappy about their choice of holiday.
   c. They would like to return to the same destination.

4. British holidaymakers often return to the same place because...
   a. they didn't do enough things the previous time.
   b. they don't like to go to places they don't know.
   c. they had such fun the first time.

5. Many British holidaymakers will have to...
   a. support the travel industry by going abroad.
   b. wait many years before travelling.
   c. comply with new rules because of the pandemic.

6. British people regret not going to certain famous places because...
   a. they enjoy going to the same place, time and again.
   b. they feel they have wasted a chance to go somewhere special.
   c. they think their partner would have liked to go.

7. British tourists feel envious when...
   a. people they know tell them of a successful holiday they had.
   b. they see people having a good time at the same resort.
   c. other holidaymakers stay at a better hotel than they do.

T/F Questions

Circle T or F for each of the following statements.

1. British tourists prefer to go on holidays to Asia rather than elsewhere. (**T** / **F**)

2. Nearly half the tourists think they will never go to the destination that they have always dreamed of. (**T** / **F**)

3. The tourist industry has been badly hit by the pandemic but is expected to bounce back soon. (**T** / **F**)

Writing Questions

Make a full sentence, using the following words.

1. Lots of British tourists (going / disappointed / on / after / feel / holiday).

_____

2. Holiday envy occurs when (hear / their friends / a wonderful / about / have enjoyed / people / holiday).

_____

Lake District

Scottish Highlands

Roman Bath

Stonehenge

Listening

Listen to the following 'Reading 2'. Fill in the correct phrase in each blank (a-e) and match the definitions below.

a. _____   b. _____   c. _____

d. _____   e. _____

1. places people like to go on holiday
2. something that reminds us of a person or event
3. continue for some distance
4. Shall we consider this?
5. two together
6. move a small boat on water
7. many years are needed

Reading 2 — Inbound Tourism – Places to go in the UK

1 Tourism is big business all over the world and Britain is no exception. There are many places in Britain that attract millions of tourists annually; Stonehenge in the west of England, built by Neolithic Britons over five thousand years ago; the ancient Roman Baths at Bath; the
5 Pennine Way, a 268 mile long national trail on the spine of hills that **(a)** the north of England to Scotland; the Lake District, surrounded by misty mountains, features Lake Windermere, Britain's largest natural lake; and the scenic beauty of north Wales or the Highlands of Scotland.

2 And there is London with its theatres, museums, churches and art
10 galleries that would **(b)** to enjoy; but let us look at a few unusual London **(c)** that most people do not know about.

3 Greenwich is famous for its naval museum and its international time line (GMT), but it also has a fan museum. Located in **(d)** restored Georgian houses it is dedicated to the history of handheld fans and the
15 craft of fan making. Afternoon tea is offered in the orangery.

4 In Limehouse on the Thames, which used to be a shipbuilding area centuries ago, you can **(e)** down the river taking in the sights at leisure.

5 Regent's Park is one of London's most beautiful parks with a famous zoo. If you hire a lodge in the zoo you can take guided tours of the animal enclosures after hours and sleep among the animals, just as if 20 you were living in the real life 'Jungle Book'.

NOTES　　　　l. 3: **Neolithic** 新石器時代の　l. 3: **Briton**（古代の）ブリトン人〔ローマ侵入当時 Great Britain 島の南部に住んでいたケルト人〕 l. 5: **spine**（土地・岩などの）突起、尾根　l. 6: **misty** 霧のかかった　l. 14: **handheld** 手で持てる、携帯用の　l. 15: **craft**〔美術や工芸の〕技術、技能　l. 15: **orangery** オレンジ栽培温室◆英国の富豪貴族の象徴

Comprehension Questions

Choose the best answer (a-c).

1. Stonehenge is a large stone structure, ...
   a. created by artists hundreds of years ago.
   b. well-known for its ancient history.
   c. visited by a few tourists each year.

2. Why do you think the baths are called the 'Roman Baths'?
   a. Because they were built in Italy.
   b. Because recently tourists from Rome enjoy bathing there.
   c. Because they were made famous during the Roman Empire.

3. The Pennine Way...
   a. is a long walking path that reaches Scotland.
   b. is the name of a road that goes up to the top of the Pennine mountain.
   c. is a running track between England and Scotland.

4. Lake Windermere is...
   a. a man-made lake covering a wide area.
   b. a large area of water.
   c. the only lake in the area surrounded by mountains.

5. To experience all the things to do in London...
   a. would take you many years.
   b. you would need a long holiday.
   c. would be a waste of energy and time.

6. Greenwich is well-known...

    a. as a place from where international time is calculated.

    b. for its pair of Georgian houses.

    c. because fans have been made there for many years.

7. What you can do at Limehouse is...

    a. build a ship and sail it down the river.

    b. walk along the river and enjoy the view.

    c. row a boat slowly down the Thames.

T/F Questions

Circle T or F for each of the following statements.

1. Tourism is not so important for the British economy. (**T** / **F**)

2. The Greenwich fan museum offers refreshments for visitors. (**T** / **F**)

3. Visitors can sleep in the animal enclosures in Regent's Park Zoo. (**T** / **F**)

Writing Questions

Make a full sentence, using the following words.

1. North Wales and the Highlands of Scotland are places of natural beauty and (attracted / foreign / each year / thousands of / are / to both places / visitors).

    _____

2. You can enjoy the excitement of sleeping in a lodge in London Zoo, (all the / around / feeling / animals / you / hearing and).

    _____

© lonndubh / Shutterstock.com
Westminster, London, UK. March 25, 2017. Anti Brexit protesters demonstrate during a march to parliament. Their banner proclaims the importance of the single market for jobs.

Chapter 9

Post Brexit Britain

ポスト・ブレグジット［英国の欧州連合離脱後］

> ブレグジットは国内で意見が二分した問題の一つだ。離脱賛成派は英国の民主的権利や自由が制限されていると感じていた。反対派は経済が受ける損失だけでなく、文化や教育等の損失も憂慮した。EU に定住した年金受給者は年金額の減少や医療給付の削減を案じている。

Reading 1 ## Warm-up

Using your dictionary, find the meanings of the following words.

1. impact
2. estimated
3. emerging
4. agreement
5. punish
6. viable
7. boost
8. much-needed

Choose the best answer (a-c).

1. What does the word 'post' mean in the title?
   a. Mail
   b. Before
   c. After

2. Brexit means...
   a. Britain leaving the EU.
   b. Britain exiting the world.
   c. Britain giving up the UN.

Is the Future of the UK in Europe?

🔊 Audio 18

1 Brexiteers (supporters of Brexit) argue that the impact of Brexit on trade, services, visas, banks and retail sales will be less than many economists fear.

2 It is estimated that in 10 years' time most global economic growth
5 will come from emerging markets, where 85% of the world's population lives; whereas, in most EU nations the population is in decline.

3 Every year for the last decade, the UK's trade with emerging markets has grown, while trade with the EU has fallen — now less than 43% of all UK exports.

10 **4** However, it is now questionable whether Britain and the EU will meet the deadline for a mutually accepted trade agreement. If they don't, then the UK and EU would have to operate by tough WTO rules which would damage trade on both sides.

5 Brexiteers say if the EU tries to 'punish' the UK by avoiding any
15 trade deal, this will harm the EU's economy more. Many large EU companies admit they need to trade with Britain on fair terms.

6 Some EU leaders are encouraging a breakup of the UK, offering to make an independent Scotland a member of the EU. If Scotland can maintain a viable economy, independence is possible.

20 **7** Undoubtedly, the UK will continue to need large numbers of migrants from all over the world to boost its economic growth, supply much-needed talent and skills, and increase its population. However, present government policy is designed to limit immigration to those with high incomes, creating major headaches for the service, tourism and
25 agricultural sectors.

NOTES　　l. 2: **retail sale** 小売販売　l. 11: **meet**〔要求・条件など〕合う、満たす◆ meet the deadline「締め切りに間に合う」　l. 11: **mutually** 互いに、相互に

Comprehension Questions

Choose the best answer (a-c).

1. What is the main message of this text?
    a. It would be better for Britain to wait before leaving the EU.
    b. Leaving the EU has possible merits and demerits for the British economy.
    c. The way forward for Britain is not to leave the EU.

2. The emerging markets include...
    a. China, Germany and Britain.
    b. Russia, India and Japan.
    c. India, China and Russia.

3. What is the percentage of Britain's non-EU exports?
    a. 57%
    b. 43%
    c. 85%

4. Britain and the EU have to work to a tight deadline to complete a mutual trade agreement. Why is this a problem?
    a. Because Brexit may not happen if they run out of time.
    b. Because both sides will have to do business by harsher rules.
    c. Because the writer is unsure if Brexit is a good idea or not.

5. What do some Brexiteers think the effect of 'punishing' the UK will be on the EU?
    a. They think it may be worse for Britain.
    b. They think that the EU can benefit.
    c. They think that it will damage the EU more.

6. Why might Scotland break away from the UK?
    a. Because its economy may be strong enough to do so.
    b. Because the people of Scotland hate the English so much.
    c. Because the EU will instruct it to do so.

7. Why is the government's policy on immigration flawed?
    a. Because British birth rates are sufficient without immigration.
    b. Because not allowing low-income immigrants will hurt the economy.
    c. Because rich immigrants boost the economy, while poor immigrants damage it.

T/F Questions

Circle T or F for each of the following statements.

1. Many economists are worried that Brexit will damage the British economy.
   (**T** / **F**)

2. Birth rates of most countries in the emerging markets are increasing compared to developed nations. (**T** / **F**)

3. Immigration will continue to have a damaging effect on the life of the British nation. (**T** / **F**)

Writing Questions

Make a full sentence, using the following words.

1. In the future Britain (the EU / will / emerging markets / on / much more / than / rely).

   _____

2. If the Scottish economy is strong enough, (from the UK / one / of Brexit / independence / possible / is / outcome).

   _____

Listening

🔊 Audio 19

Listen to the following 'Reading 2'. Fill in the correct phrase in each blank (a-e) and match the definitions below.

a. ⬚⬚⬚⬚⬚⬚⬚   b. ⬚⬚⬚⬚⬚⬚⬚   c. ⬚⬚⬚⬚⬚⬚⬚

d. ⬚⬚⬚⬚⬚⬚⬚   e. ⬚⬚⬚⬚⬚⬚⬚

1. increases connected to price rises
2. applied to a doctor for medical care
3. increases each year
4. do not have enough money to pay for something
5. somebody pays for this
6. asking for a refund
7. the prices of daily items in shops, etc.

Reading 2 — Uncertainty for Pensioners Living Abroad

1 A total of 1.2 million UK citizens live abroad in the EU. Many of these are pensioners receiving the same **(a)** as those in Britain. Such rises are denied to pensioners living in most non-EU countries, including Japan.

2 About 310,000 UK citizens have migrated to Spain, 106,610 of whom are state pensioners. The sunny climate, sandy beaches and the lower **(b)** are powerful attractions. 5

3 But Brexit now threatens the future of the pensioner abroad. The pound's fall against the euro has already hit the value of the pension. Britain's withdrawal may also mean the end of the **(c)** that pensioners inside the EU presently enjoy. 10

4 Another concern is healthcare, because there is a huge imbalance between British pensioners using EU health services and EU pensioners using the NHS. In Spain 70,000 retired UK citizens use Spain's doctors and hospitals. In the UK only 81 Spanish pensioners registered for treatment by the NHS. 15

5 As a member of the European Economic Area (the EU plus Norway, Iceland and Liechtenstein) health costs are covered by the migrant's

home nation. The UK paid £674.4m in health bills to other EEA countries in 2014-15 and (d) only £49.7m. Having left the EU, the UK
20 government could cut this health provision to save money.

6 Sir Roger Gale, an MP and pension campaigner, said, "the victims include a lot of very elderly, very frail people. They cannot sell their homes at the price they paid for them, and they (e) the inflated house prices or rents in Britain." They are trapped.

NOTES   l. 8: **euro**《通貨単位》ユーロ◆ EU 諸国に導入された統一通貨。1 ユーロは 100（ユーロ）セントに下位区分される。   l. 20: **provision** 供給、提供   l. 22: **frail**〔人や体が〕病弱な

Comprehension Questions

Choose the best answer (a-c).

1. Why did so many British pensioners decide to live abroad in the EU?
    a. Because they wanted to find a better job than in the UK.
    b. Because they wanted to enjoy a rising pension and better weather.
    c. Because they wanted to experience free movement all over the world.

2. How many British pensioners live in Spain?
    a. About a million
    b. Around 300,000
    c. Roughly 100,000

3. Why is Spain one of the most popular places for UK pensioners to live?
    a. It has a better medical system than the UK.
    b. It has a more pleasant climate than Britain.
    c. It has a similar culture and language as in the UK.

4. What are the two dangers UK pensioners living abroad face from Brexit?
    a. Having their pension frozen and likely increased health costs.
    b. The falling value of the pound and worsening local weather.
    c. Losing private health insurance and their state pension.

5. What condition does Sir Roger Gale say many of these retirees are in?
    a. They are getting sick because of the foreign food.
    b. They are old and not in good health.
    c. They want to return to their families in the UK.

6. How does Sir Roger Gale describe their financial situation?

   a. They have lost money by speculating on Spanish property.

   b. Most of their money is in bank accounts earning low interest.

   c. They will lose money if they sell their home.

7. If these British pensioners return to the UK what problems do they face?

   a. They will not be able to afford to live in the UK.

   b. They will find it difficult to adjust to British customs.

   c. They will have to live on a fixed state pension that will not rise.

T/F Questions

Circle T or F for each of the following statements.

1. The members of the EEA are the same as those of the EU. (**T** / **F**)

2. British retirees living in Japan on the British state pension receive regular increases. (**T** / **F**)

3. Under the EEA agreement the patient's nation pays the host country for health care costs. (**T** / **F**)

Writing Questions

Make a full sentence, using the following words.

1. British pensioners (and low cost / of its sunny climate, / to Spain / because / have migrated / sandy beaches / of living).

   _____

2. Britain may (living / to cut / in the EU / want / health costs / the high / of British citizens).

   _____

© Oleh Dubyna / Shutterstock.com
KHARKIV, UKRAINE–18 SEPTEMBER 2019: English
professional footballer Kyle Walker during UEFA Champions
League match Shakhtar–Manchester City at Metalist Stadium

Chapter 10

Leisure & Sport in the UK

レジャーとスポーツ

> 英国では仕事は人生に楽しみを与えてくれるものではなく、生活のために仕方のないものと考える人が多い。その点、専業主婦は TV やジムを楽しむ「レジャー・クィーン」である。一方、英国で最も人気のあるスポーツはフットボールだが、時に社会問題となり、その価値に疑問が持たれることもある。

Reading 1 ▶ ## Warm-up

Using your dictionary, find the meanings of the following words.

1. conversely   **2.** gym rat   **3.** overwhelming   **4.** classify

5. oddly   **6.** glue (v)   **7.** colossal   **8.** obesity

Choose the best answer (a-c).

1. What do you think the title "Leisure Queens" means?

   a. The British Queen has a lot of free time.

   b. Housewives who spend time looking after their family.

   c. Women in Britain have many hours to enjoy themselves.

2. Leisure Queens...

   a. prefer to use their time creatively.

   b. spend time mostly on their career.

   c. watch too much television.

Reading 1 | Leisure Queens

🔊 Audio 20

1 British women have more free time than those in Europe says a recent survey and they spend most of it in front of the TV. The average woman in Britain spends five and a half hours relaxing each day according to the Organisation for Economic Co-operation and Development (OECD). As many career women in Britain have to bring 5 up children and also have to hold down a job, this figure is surprising.

2 According to the report British women at home spend much of their leisure time watching TV, more than two hours each day. Conversely, they spend just under 20 minutes each day on sport; but apart from the rare gym rat an overwhelming majority probably do nothing. 10

3 Oddly, the report classifies child care as 'unpaid work.' However, many mothers with a career would disagree and say that it should be classified as "leisure time." Therefore, women at home actually have longer than five and a half hours of leisure.

4 British women who stay at home and are glued to the TV each day, 15 are wasting a colossal amount of time and their own talent. It might be better for them to do something more useful like reading a book, joining volunteer activities, going to a museum, working in the garden, or learning to play a musical instrument.

5 In addition, Britain's children are not doing well in educational 20 achievement tables and obesity among young people is on the rise. By watching so much TV this survey suggests that British housewives are not setting the best example for their children.

NOTES   l. 6: **hold down**〔職に〕就いている   l. 21: **on the rise** 増加して（いる）

Comprehension Questions

1. A recent survey has found that British women...
   a. have more leisure time than other women in the world.
   b. have more free time than those in Europe.
   c. watch TV and don't have children.

2. The OECD has found that British women spend...
   a. more than five hours at leisure.
   b. less than five hours enjoying free time.
   c. around half the day watching TV.

3. Women in Britain...
   a. watch TV more than doing anything else.
   b. watch TV for nearly half their leisure time.
   c. watch TV for a few minutes each day.

4. The writer states that...
   a. British women go to the gym regularly.
   b. British women don't spend much time in the gym.
   c. British women workout like rats in the gym.

5. How does the OECD classify child care?
   a. It is a hobby.
   b. It is leisure.
   c. It is unpaid work.

6. What does the writer think about spending a lot of time watching TV?
   a. It is an educational and stimulating activity.
   b. It is something that should be done over a long time period.
   c. It is unproductive and useless.

7. Which activity is not listed up by the writer as one of the useful activities?
   a. Learning to play the piano
   b. Working at a charity shop
   c. Going to the gym

T/F Questions

Circle T or F for each of the following statements.

1. It is strange that British women who are often busy with work or children have so much time for themselves. (**T / F**)

2. The statistics show that British women frequently go to the gym and workout for more than 20 minutes each day. (**T / F**)

3. British women could help their children more if they watched less TV. (**T / F**)

Writing Questions

Make a full sentence, using the following words.

1. The leisure time that British women enjoy (of / much greater / that / in Europe / than / is / other women).

_____

2. Other than watching television (worthwhile pursuits / there are / undertake / British women / many other / could / that).

_____

© Silvi Photo
London, UK - March 16 2019: Declan Rice of West Ham United during the Premier League match between West Ham United and Huddersfield Town at the London Stadium, Queen Elizabeth Olympic Park

Listening

Listen to the following 'Reading 2'. Fill in the correct phrase in each blank (a-e) and match the definitions below.

a. ▨▨▨▨▨▨▨▨   b. ▨▨▨▨▨▨▨▨   c. ▨▨▨▨▨▨▨▨

d. ▨▨▨▨▨▨▨▨   e. ▨▨▨▨▨▨▨▨

1. violent behavior
2. very important for something
3. rules are fixed
4. made worse
5. time for the mid-day meal
6. all over the world
7. good times and bad

FOOTBALL

Reading 2   Football in Britain

1 Football is enormously popular in the UK, more so than rugby and cricket. The national teams are England, Wales, Scotland and Northern Ireland. Although, football probably began in England in the 12th century it didn't **(a)** until the creation of the Football Association in 1863.
5 The first international match was in 1872 when England played Scotland.

2 There are now over 40,000 registered football clubs in England. The biggest names are in the Premier League and they attract millions of supporters from **(b)**.

10 **3** And it's not just about men. Women's football now attracts 34% of British adults, according to new research.

4 Football (called soccer in Japan) is attractive because it is so simple to play. Only a ball and a few players are needed. Kids play it after school or office workers in their **(c)**. It's a good way to make friends and, after
15 practice, players often visit a pub for a few pints.

5 Although professional clubs often ban alcohol at matches, hooliganism among fans, fuelled by drinking, can sometimes be a problem.

6 But fans **(d)** the game. Fans choose their team early in life and they stick with it through **(e)**, going to games, cheering on their team and singing songs as loudly as possible.

7 Sadly, some young fans have become addicted to gambling on the results of matches. The government says it aims to tackle this social problem by prohibiting betting companies from being sponsors of teams and stopping their names appearing on players' shirts.

NOTES   l. 15: **pint** 《液量単位》パイント◆＝〈英〉0.568 リットル＝約 500cc   l. 19: **stick with ...** 〜にこだわる、〜の一点張りで通す

Comprehension Questions

Choose the best answer (a-c).

1. In the UK, football...

 a. is nearly as popular as rugby and cricket.

 b. is one of the most popular sports after rugby and cricket.

 c. is a more popular sport than rugby and cricket.

2. The British National Football Team...

 a. does not exist.

 b. is the top team in the world.

 c. doesn't include Scotland, Wales and Northern Ireland.

3. There are...

 a. 40,000 teams in the Premier League.

 b. a few hundred teams throughout the UK.

 c. millions of fans of the top British teams throughout the world.

4. Women's football in the UK...

 a. is now supported by more than a third of adults.

 b. is not as popular as it was amongst adults.

 c. is supported by more adult women than men.

5. Football is popular partly because...

 a. it is called 'soccer' in Japan.

 b. it is simple to play.

 c. it is played by office workers and kids.

6. One positive aspect of amateur football is that...

    a. players can get drunk after practice.

    b. players can make friends through the game.

    c. players can easily become professionals.

7. One of the negative aspects of professional football is that...

    a. fans get violent under the influence of alcohol.

    b. fans cannot buy alcohol at matches and become violent.

    c. violence by fans at matches is increasing because of a lack of alcohol.

T/F Questions

Circle T or F for each of the following statements.

1. Before the creation of the Football Association, football was not played in the UK. (**T** / **F**)

2. Becoming a fan of a club is something that starts early in life and rarely changes. (**T** / **F**)

3. The government is ignoring the problem of fans gambling on the results of football matches. (**T** / **F**)

Writing Questions

Make a full sentence, using the following words.

1. One of the ways of discouraging gambling at (from / to ban / club sponsors / is / football matches / gambling companies / becoming).

    _____

2. Football is not just for men, (has become / women's soccer / popular / is / and / enormously / established).

    _____

Chapter 11

The British Empire

大英帝国

> 英国は世界に類を見ない大帝国であった。アメリカやインド、アフリカの広範囲が含まれた。現代の研究ではこの歴史には恥ずべき事がたくさんあるとしているが、多くの英国人は帝国時代は良かったと考えている。香港でも人々は王室だけでなく民主的な統治に郷愁を感じている。

Reading 1 ▶ Warm-up

Using your dictionary, find the meanings of the following words.

1. documentary
2. colourful
3. background
4. positive
5. infrastructure
6. govern
7. colony
8. promote

Choose the best answer (a-c).

1. What is the symbol of the British Empire?
   a. A horse
   b. A lion
   c. A tiger

2. The word 'survey' has the same meaning as...
   a. TV programme.
   b. newspaper.
   c. questionnaire.

🔊 Audio 22

1 British people have often found it difficult to agree on whether Britain's former empire was good or bad. There are documentary TV programmes that try to show what life was like
5 for people in those countries under the British. There are also colourful dramas that use the empire as a background to stories of romance and adventure. But what do the British really think of it? Well, the British government did a
10 survey to find out.

2 Among the British public, feelings tend to be positive. A YouGov survey found that most think the British Empire is more something to be proud of rather than ashamed of. The
15 survey also found that young people are least likely to feel pride in the empire. About two-thirds of over 60s feel mostly proud.

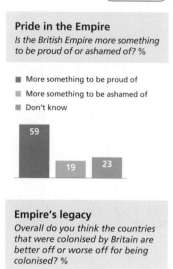

Pride in the Empire
Is the British Empire more something to be proud of or ashamed of? %

■ More something to be proud of
■ More something to be ashamed of
■ Don't know

59 19 23

Empire's legacy
Overall do you think the countries that were colonised by Britain are better off or worse off for being colonised? %

■ Better off
■ Worse off
■ Don't know

49 15 36

3 The British Empire invested in infrastructure, started new trading routes and set up schools, hospitals and local government – but it also
20 took away resources, failed to stop famines and it left some countries unprepared to govern. Though many are unsure, British people do seem to think that, overall, former British colonies are now better off for having been part of the empire rather than worse off.

4 Other statistics show a third of British people would like it if Britain
25 still had an empire. Under half say they would not like the empire to exist today. Nearly a quarter don't know.

5 The Commonwealth is made up of the nations of the former British Empire, and promotes the interests of those countries, through trade agreements and sports events.

NOTES   l. 20: **take away** 奪い去る   l. 20: **left** < leave ある状態のままにしておく   l. 22: **overall** 《副》全般的に見れば   l. 22: **better off** 〔～した方が〕一層暮らし向きが良くなる、いっそう裕福である   l. 23: **worse off** 暮らしが悪くなる、より困窮している

Comprehension Questions

Choose the best answer (a-c).

1. Why did the British government decide to do a survey?

    a. To encourage people to be proud of the British Empire

    b. To make it easier for people to agree on the British Empire

    c. To discover what people think about the British Empire

2. Where do many British people get their ideas on empire from?

    a. The government

    b. TV programmes

    c. Surveys

3. Find the correct information from the chart.

    a. 19% proud

    b. 59% ashamed

    c. 23% don't know

4. What is the difference between how young people and old people feel about the British Empire?

    a. Young people are prouder of the British Empire.

    b. Older people are prouder of the British Empire.

    c. Young and old people are equally unsure about the British Empire.

5. What positive things did the British Empire do?

    a. It helped the colonies to develop.

    b. It successfully stopped famines.

    c. It prepared all the colonies to govern themselves.

6. What % of British people believe former British colonies were better off under the British Empire?

    a. 15%

    b. 49%

    c. 36%

7. How many people say they would like Britain to have an empire today?

    a. Under half

    b. Over half

    c. Exactly half

T/F Questions

1. The Commonwealth exists to help poor countries. (**T** / **F**)

2. The British Government did not want to find out what British people felt. (**T** / **F**)

3. Generally speaking, British people think the empire was a good thing. (**T** / **F**)

Writing Questions

Make a full sentence, using the following words.

1. The British Empire is (strong / that / opinions on / British people / a subject / many / have).

   _____

2. Generally, people get (TV / on the / their / British Empire / ideas / watching / from).

   _____

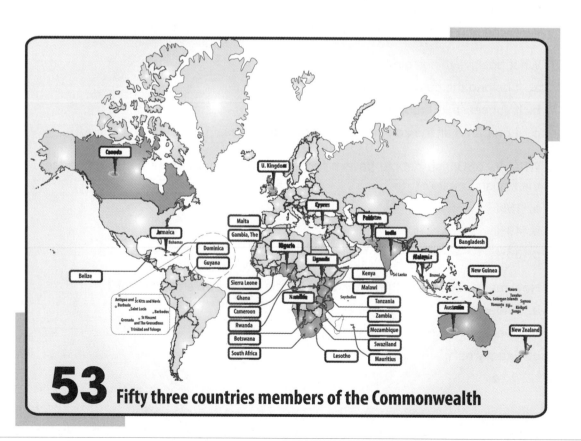

53 Fifty three countries members of the Commonwealth

Listening 🔊 **Audio 23**

Listen to the following 'Reading 2'. Fill in the correct phrase in each blank (a-e) and match the definitions below.

a. ▭▭▭▭▭▭   b. ▭▭▭▭▭▭   c. ▭▭▭▭▭▭

d. ▭▭▭▭▭▭   e. ▭▭▭▭▭▭

1. attracted many people
2. has a lot of aspects
3. reflect on the past
4. something which cannot be answered
5. even though it is true
6. 150 years
7. controlling one's own opinions

Reading 2   Nostalgia for the British Empire in Hong Kong

1 The wedding of Britain's Prince Harry and American actress Meghan Markle in London **(a)** in far away Hong Kong. This seems to be unexplainable, until you think about Britain's colonial rule. After all, Hong Kong was a British colony for over a century and a half.

2 More than two decades after reunification with China, a growing number of Hongkongers are **(b)** British rule with nostalgia. More and more people are saying that life was better under the British.   5

3 They complain that under the new system they have to live in

© Blueskynet / Shutterstock.com
Windsor, Berkshire / United Kingdom – May 19th 2018: Harry and Meghan's wedding

© Jimmy Siu / Shutterstock.com
Hong Kong – 1 Jan 2020: A million attend demo, demand universal suffrage, 2020 direct democratic elections for Legislative Council without functional constituency

tiny subdivided flats, their salaries have not increased, they have less
10 freedom and there is media **(c)**. Under the British, they also say, young
people were full of hope for the future, not disappointed as they feel now.
Some people feel that British rule gave them more liberty than they
have with the present Hong Kong government.

4 The legacy of the British Empire is **(d)**, including the English
15 language, parliamentary politics, the rule of law, an independent
judiciary and the separation of powers.

5 Recently in Hong Kong there have been many huge and violent
demonstrations against the Hong Kong government. Demonstrators feel
their rights are being taken away because of the influence of China.

20 **6** These young students have appealed to the rest of the world to help
them in their fight. When America showed support for them the
democracy demonstrators were happy that the strongest nation in the
world was behind them, **(e)** that Britain had supported them, too.
Clearly, Britain is a faded power. The broken promise made by China of
25 "one country, two systems" is eroding the British legacy of democratic
governance.

NOTES   l. 5: **reunification** 再統合、再統一   l. 9: **subdivided** 再分割された   l. 15: **parliamentary** 議会の
l. 24: **faded** 衰えた、弱まった

Comprehension Questions

Choose the best answer (a-c).

1. Why was the British royal wedding so popular in Hong Kong?
   a. Because Hongkongers like weddings.
   b. Because Hong Kong was part of the British Empire for a long time.
   c. Because the royal couple visited Hong Kong and were popular.

2. What happened over 20 years ago?
   a. Hong Kong was reunited with China.
   b. Hong Kong was made independent.
   c. Hong Kong was given back to Britain.

3. How do many Hongkongers feel about their situation now?
   a. They feel they have a better life than under the British.
   b. They think that life was good when they were in the British Empire.
   c. They prefer to have a quiet life under the Chinese.

4. Why do many Hongkongers think the legacy of the British Empire is important?

   a. Because it gave them laws to live by.

   b. Because they like the royal family.

   c. Because they can live peacefully now.

5. Why are young people demonstrating in Hong Kong?

   a. They want a more democratic society.

   b. They have free time to make trouble on the streets.

   c. They want to be part of the UK again.

6. Which is the most powerful country in the world now, according to the text?

   a. China

   b. Britain

   c. America

7. Why is the influence of the British Empire still important to Hongkongers?

   a. It protects them from China.

   b. It taught them the principles of freedom and law.

   c. It gave them an English education.

T/F Questions

Circle T or F for each of the following statements.

1. Britain is the strongest power in the world. (**T** / **F**)

2. Hongkongers feel that the British Empire was good for them. (**T** / **F**)

3. There have been many demonstrations in support of the Chinese government. (**T** / **F**)

Writing Questions

Make a full sentence, using the following words.

1. The interest in (is connected / of Hong Kong / Britain's / the royal wedding / rule / to / long).

   _____

2. Young (less / future / about / confident / feel / their / Hongkongers).

   _____

© Anton Garin

Media in the UK

英国のメディア

> 人々はスマートフォンやコンピュータから必要な情報を集める。現実に背を向け、長時間スクリーンを凝視する子供に、親たちは心配を隠せない。サイバー上のいじめやフェイク・ニュースは大丈夫か。近年 BBC は「公正でわかりやすいニュースを配信していない」と批判されている。

Reading 1 ▶ ## Warm-up

Using your dictionary, find the meanings of the following words.

1. equate
2. peril
3. poll (v)
4. sleep-deprived
5. victim
6. intimidate
7. reveal
8. vent

Choose the best answer (a-c).

1. What is a social networking site?

   a. A virtual place where you can meet friends and chat

   b. A shopping centre where you can buy all kinds of goods

   c. A computer café where you can learn about the Internet

2. What do you think this text will discuss?

   a. The good and bad points of Internet use

   b. The merits and demerits of using a computer

   c. The plus and minus points of keyboards

Reading 1　Social Networking–Positives and Negatives

🔊 Audio 24

1 In the UK there are now 45 million social media users. This equates to 67% of the entire population. Of these, 39 million are mobile social media users. The largest is Facebook, with over 32,000,000 users in the UK, closely followed by Twitter (20 million), YouTube and LinkedIn (19 million). 5

2 Millions of people use social media sites for both work and pleasure. Social networking is a topic that divides opinion – some people think it's an amazing tool but others are worried about the impact it has on people's lives. Staying safe online and the perils of Twitter 'addiction' are hot topics now. 10

3 Pupils at a London school recently polled parents and teachers to get their views on social networking. The survey found that 37% of those questioned say they are sleep-deprived as a result of social networking. Respondents are also worried about cyber-bullying. Unfortunately, the only way for bullies to be stopped is if they are reported, but victims may 15 be too intimidated to do so. Many say social networking can also be a waste of time as people end up spending the whole day 'in front of the screen' without achieving anything useful.

4 However, on the other hand, the survey revealed that people feel they can express themselves, and relieve mental stress, by venting their 20 feelings online. It is also a lot easier to keep in touch with family and friends, especially if they live far away.

5 However, cautious use of the Internet is vital because a huge amount of users' private information is available to public view.

NOTES　　l. 17: **end up (by) doing** 結局〜になる、〜することになる　l. 23: **cautious** 注意深い

Comprehension Questions

Choose the best answer (a-c).

1. Social media in the UK is being used by...
   a. the entire population of Britain.
   b. around two thirds of British people.
   c. just under 40 million people.

2. Mobile social media users account for...
   a. more than 85% of the social media users in the country.
   b. a small percentage of social media usage worldwide.
   c. those who use computers at home as well.

3. There are millions of people who use social media for...
   a. fun and socialization but not for chatting with friends.
   b. finding out what their friends are doing, exclusively.
   c. making contact with friends and also doing work-related things.

4. Many people in Britain are concerned about...
   a. not getting up on time in the morning.
   b. the problem of becoming addicted to SNS.
   c. being safe when going out in the street.

5. The information concerning social networking in this text comes from...
   a. research conducted by a media company.
   b. a poll carried out through a social media research center.
   c. a survey done by students at a school.

6. Two social networking problems that came out of the survey were...
   a. cyber bullying and sleep deprivation.
   b. wasting time on the Internet and making too many friends.
   c. not getting enough sleep and being bullied by teachers at school.

7. The advantages of social networking are that you can...
   a. avoid your friends and keep in touch with your family.
   b. get outside to enjoy the day and relieve stress.
   c. easily contact friends and family and express yourself online.

T/F Questions

Circle T or F for each of the following statements.

1. British people mostly have similar views about the value of the Internet. (**T / F**)

2. The most popular social media tool in the UK is Facebook, by a wide margin. (**T / F**)

3. Because social media sites store a lot of users' personal data, it is better to be safe than sorry. (**T / F**)

Writing Questions

Make a full sentence, using the following words.

1. The only way to stop a cyber bully is (to the authorities / frightened / to report / to do so / him or her / may be / but the victim).

   _____

2. It is important to be very careful online (visible / user / because / information / our private / may be / to any other).

   _____

© Kim Lewis Photography / Shutterstock.com
London, England/UK–March 29, 2019: Protesters gather outside Parliament to protest Brexit. One person is holding a sign that says "BBC Fake News Fake Views".

Listen to the following 'Reading 2'. Fill in the correct phrase in each blank (a-e) and match the definitions below.

a. ▨▨▨▨▨▨▨▨▨▨   b. ▨▨▨▨▨▨▨▨▨▨   c. ▨▨▨▨▨▨▨▨▨▨

d. ▨▨▨▨▨▨▨▨▨▨   e. ▨▨▨▨▨▨▨▨▨▨

1. hiding from the public
2. based on a commitment
3. not successful in doing something
4. frequently criticized
5. at that time
6. the wishes and beliefs
7. even though this idea was expressed

Reading 2   The BBC's Reporting – Is it Impartial?

1 In 1927 when Sir John Reith became the first Director General of the BBC, he stated that impartiality and objectivity were the essence of professionalism in broadcasting. **(a)**, the BBC is frequently attacked for its lack of impartial and objective journalism.

5 **2** The BBC has been criticized for everything from covering up racism, homophobia and sexual abuse to anti-Israel bias, Indophobia, inaccuracy and ineptitude. Politicians and the rest of the media have targeted the mandatory licence fee as unfair competition and the corporation **(b)** waste and over-staffing.

10 **3** Tom Mills, an academic at Aston University, argues that BBC journalists are not trusted by the people because they report issues from **(c)** of the powerful people in society. His research posits that the BBC's reporting is, 'strongly shaped by corporate interests, state officials and the political elite – the government **(d)**, in particular. Ultimately, it is 15 not accountable to the public, nor to parliament but to the government.'

4 Reporting Brexit is a big problem for BBC journalists because there is no elite consensus. Most officials, business executives and independent experts are opposed to Brexit while the population is fairly evenly split. The Conservative government was elected (e) of getting Brexit done but 'Remainers' strongly criticize the BBC for failing to challenge [20] misinformation and misconduct by Brexit campaigners.

5 The government is currently planning to reform the BBC to better serve its purposes. If this happens the BBC may lose all credibility as an impartial and objective broadcaster.

NOTES   l. 2: **impartiality** 公平性   l. 5: **cover up** 〔罪・事実・本心などを〕隠す   l. 6: **inaccuracy** 不正確な発言 [記述・陳述]   l. 7: **ineptitude** 不適当な行為 [言葉]   l. 7: **rest of** ～のその他の部分   l. 8: **mandatory** 〔法令または規則による〕強制的な   l. 12: **posit** ～と断定する、結論を下す   l. 13: **<be> shaped by** ～の影響を受けて（形作られて）いる   l. 13: **interest** 利害   l. 17: **consensus** 意見の一致   l. 18: **split** 分裂した   l. 21: **misconduct** 違法 [不正] 行為

Chapter 12 : Media in the UK

Comprehension Questions

Choose the best answer (a-c).

1. The first Director General of the BBC...
    a. outlined the fundamental principles of broadcasting.
    b. made it clear that the BBC was serving the interests of the government.
    c. was careful to avoid giving an opinion.

2. The BBC is often criticized for not being impartial...
    a. in spite of the opinion of the founding Director General that balanced reporting was not necessary.
    b. even though the first Director General said it was essential in broadcasting.
    c. because BBC journalists of today continue to follow the principles of the original Director General.

3. Criticism of the BBC includes two issues of concern:...
    a. disapproval of the state of India and lack of journalistic accuracy.
    b. a lack of professionalism and support of the state of Israel.
    c. in-depth coverage of racism and inept reporting.

4. A frequent criticism of the BBC is...
    a. the careful way in which the corporation is managed.
    b. the low fees paid to staff at the corporation.
    c. the licence fee, which is seen as unfair.

5. The argument made by Tom Mills, based on his research, is that bias in the BBC...

   a. is caused by its close identity with the government.

   b. is a problem of corruption amongst journalists.

   c. has occurred because ordinary people have too much influence on the corporation.

6. The results of research at Aston University show that...

   a. the central government has too much influence on the BBC.

   b. the BBC is continuing to pursue its goals of impartiality and objectivity.

   c. the BBC has achieved a reporting balance that is disliked by all its users.

7. Brexit is an issue that is particularly difficult for the BBC because...

   a. no-one agrees on what should be done.

   b. the population is in favour of Brexit by a large margin.

   c. top business people and experts are against it while the government is for it.

T/F Questions

Circle T or F for each of the following statements.

1. The BBC was strongly criticized for ignoring misconduct by Brexit campaigners. (**T** / **F**)

2. The BBC will be allowed to continue in its present form by the government. (**T** / **F**)

3. The present government wants to control the BBC more. (**T** / **F**)

Writing Questions

Make a full sentence, using the following words.

1. Nearly a hundred years ago at the founding of the BBC (were / of impartiality / by its / the principles / and objectivity / leader / set out).

   _____

2. Now is an extremely critical time for the BBC because its future role is being evaluated by the government (the reporting / is being / and / of its / questioned / journalists).

   _____

UNITED KINGDOM

Chapter *13*

Regions of Britain

英国の 4 つの地域

> 英国は 4 つの地域から成り立っている。イングランド、スコットランド、ウェールズ、そして北アイルランドだ。ブレグジットはスコットランドの独立の気運を高めた。イングランドは中でも最大の地域であり、それ自体も、経済や文化や方言の面から北と南で線引きされる。

Reading 1 ▶ Warm-up

Using your dictionary, find the meanings of the following words.

1. autonomy
2. devolution
3. reserve
4. derive
5. edge
6. remain
7. unite (v)
8. eventuality

Choose the best answer (a-c).

1. Britain is a...
   a. country divided into many parts that fight each other.
   b. state that comprises a number of regions.
   c. nation that has few regional differences.

2. Ireland is...
   a. a country made up of Northern and Southern Ireland.
   b. a country divided by religious differences.
   c. an independent nation.

1 The UK, a single sovereign state, is made up of England, Scotland, Wales and Northern Ireland. The latter three regions have gained some autonomy through a process of devolution. They each have their own assemblies where they can decide on general matters such as education
5 but the UK parliament reserves the right to deal with others such as the military.

2 The Scottish, Welsh and Irish peoples were not originally English-speaking, but Celtic. The Celtic languages were spoken all over the British Isles when the Romans arrived in 43 AD. English derives from
10 the languages spoken by the Saxon invaders who came after the Romans left around the end of the fourth century. The Saxons pushed the Celtic peoples to the northern and western edges of the British Isles. So, some Celts still think of the English as the enemy.

3 The Anglo-Normans invaded the island of Ireland in the 12th century
15 and started 800 years of English rule. Ireland was originally Catholic but Protestants from Britain settled in Northern Ireland from the 17th century, forming a strong presence. Catholic Ireland in the south fought against British rule and finally separated from Britain in 1922. Northern Ireland remained British, but Catholic and Protestant militant groups
20 continued to fight each other until the Belfast (Good Friday) Agreement brought peace in 1998.

4 Because of Brexit the Scottish government is pushing for independence while the Republic of Ireland and Northern Ireland may unite again. However, the British government is against these
25 eventualities, as they would signal the end of the 'UK.'

NOTES   l. 1: **sovereign** 主権を有する   l. 4: **assembly** 議会   l. 10: **invader** 侵略者   l. 25: **signal** ～の前兆となる、～を示す

Comprehension Questions

Choose the best answer (a-c).

1. Britain is made up of...
   a. four sovereign nation states that can make all their own decisions.
   b. four regions, three of which have some autonomy.
   c. four regions that cannot make any of their own decisions.

2. The Celtic languages...
   a. were spoken all over the UK until recently.
   b. were brought to England by the Romans.
   c. were the original languages of Britain when the Romans came.

3. The English language...
   a. is of Saxon origin, brought over by invading tribes.
   b. derives from the Latin language given to Britain by the Romans.
   c. has Celtic roots and was spoken by the original British people.

4. To this day some Celts do not trust the English, because...
   a. the Saxons were their enemy for hundreds of years.
   b. the Saxons helped the Romans to oppress the Celtic tribes.
   c. the Celts think the English are rude by refusing to speak Celtic.

5. The whole of Ireland was part of Britain until...
   a. the 12th century.
   b. the 20th century.
   c. 1998.

6. Northern Ireland became a Protestant region because...
   a. Protestant settlers arrived there in large numbers.
   b. priests persuaded the locals to switch religions.
   c. visitors to the area were mostly Protestants.

7. There was a lot of violence in Northern Ireland until 1998 because...
   a. there was a great deal of poverty and crime.
   b. Protestants and local Catholics fought for independence.
   c. people fought each other over religious and political differences.

T/F Questions

1. The Scottish Parliament has committed itself to challenge the UK government over independence. (**T** / **F**)

2. The Celtic speaking nations are going to take control of Britain. (**T** / **F**)

3. Independence for Scotland and re-unification of Ireland are matters that the British government opposes. (**T** / **F**)

Writing Questions

Make a full sentence, using the following words.

1. The language that was spoken by the original inhabitants of (the Roman occupation / English / was / before / the British Isles / not).

   _____

2. Independence for Scotland would mean that the United Kingdom (cease to / and after that / simply 'Great Britain' / would probably / would / be called / exist).

   _____

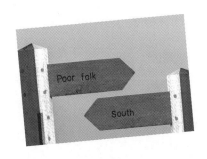

North of England

South of England

Reading 2 ▶ ## Listening

🔊 **Audio 27**

Listen to the following 'Reading 2'. Fill in the correct phrase in each blank (a-e) and match the definitions below.

a. ▩▩▩▩▩▩▩   b. ▩▩▩▩▩▩▩   c. ▩▩▩▩▩▩▩

d. ▩▩▩▩▩▩▩   e. ▩▩▩▩▩▩▩

1. to be richer
2. the area in the centre of England
3. non-standard 'a' 'e' 'i' 'o' 'u' sounds
4. to look down on others by laughing
5. a person's age between 37 and 39
6. the average age at which people die
7. welcome people

Reading 2   ## England, North & South–A Divided Nation?

1 According to a new study by experts at Liverpool University the north of England officially starts in Leicestershire, which shocked many people living there who thought they were Midlanders.

2 However, my mother would not be shocked. She was born in Leicester and firmly believed that the people of **(a)** and the north had the same character; they work hard and are friendly while in the south they are lazy and rude. She moved to the south coast in her **(b)** and lived there most of her life, but her stereotypical views never changed.

3 Not only that, she didn't change the way she spoke, either. Leicester, or anywhere north of it, is where people use the short 'a' for 'grass' and 'glass' as in 'cat', whereas in the south people use the long 'a' as in 'smart'. After we moved 'down south' schoolmates would **(c)** my 'funny' vowels, so I changed my pronunciation to that of the south. Though, whenever I visit the Midlands my original accent returns.

4 Economically, no doubt the south is **(d)** than the north. Southerners earn more than northerners on average; unemployment is around 50% higher in the north; average house prices in the south east are nearly double those of the north; school pupils in the south are 40% more likely to receive higher grades in national exams than northerners; and **(e)** in the south is around 15% higher than the north.

20

5 The research shows my bigoted mum was right about one thing; northerners are more likely to be friendly and greet visitors with a smile.

NOTES   l. 7: **lazy** 怠惰な   l. 8: **stereotypical** 型にはまった   l. 9: **not only that,** そればかりでなく◆文副詞句   l. 13: **vowel** 母音   l. 21: **bigoted** 〔他人の意見に耳を傾けず〕凝り固まった考えを持つ、頑固な

Comprehension Questions

Choose the best answer (a-c).

1. Leicester was traditionally part of...
    a. the Midlands.
    b. the North.
    c. the South.

2. The author's mother...
    a. had strong views about the people of the north and south.
    b. moved to the south because she liked southern people.
    c. thought the people of the south were kind and hard-working.

3. English spoken in the north of England...
    a. is the same as the way people speak it in the south.
    b. has some significant vowel differences from the south.
    c. is a different language from that of the south.

4. Recent statistics show that...
    a. people in the north earn more than those in the south.
    b. people in the south have a higher income than those in the north.
    c. there is little difference in salaries between the two regions.

5. The unemployment rate...
    a. is much higher in the north than in the south.
    b. is quite similar between the two regions.
    c. is slightly lower in the north than in the south.

6. It is cheaper to buy a house...

   a. in the south east than in the north.

   b. in the north than in the south.

   c. in the south than in the north.

7. If you live in the south...

   a. your national test scores will likely be better.

   b. your motivation to study will be stronger.

   c. your teachers will be less well qualified.

T/F Questions

Circle T or F for each of the following statements.

1. You are likely to live longer if you live in the south than in the north. (**T** / **F**)

2. The author's mother was totally wrong in her opinions about people from the north. (**T** / **F**)

3. The survey found out something new about where the north actually starts in England. (**T** / **F**)

Writing Questions

Make a full sentence, using the following words.

1. According to the results of the research it is clear that (and Midlands / from the north / friendlier / are / of the south / the people / than those).

   _____

2. Despite living in the south for many years (never / of the south / her views / the writer's / about the people / mother / changed).

   _____

A clergyman and a dog

Chapter *14*

God & a Dog

神様と犬

> 英国はキリスト教の国であるが、異なる宗教を持つ移民が入ってきている。例えば、イスラム教徒が増加している。また、宗教を信じない人々も増えてきている。日常生活では物乞いをする路上生活者に目を引かれる。この問題の解決には地方自治体とチャリティの協力が必要だ。

Reading 1 ▶ Warm-up

Using your dictionary, find the meanings of the following words.

1. proportion　　2. predict　　3. expansion　　4. atheist
5. significant　　6. realignment　　7. de-christianisation　　8. bloodshed

Choose the best answer (a-c).

1. What do you think the following article is about?
   a. Fewer and fewer people believe in Christianity.
   b. The Christian religion is getting more extreme in the UK.
   c. Muslim people will become Christians in the future.

2. What is the change that will happen to religion in the UK?
   a. The Muslim religion will challenge Christianity.
   b. Television will take over as the major religion.
   c. Non-believers in God will be in the majority.

Christianity–A Minority Religion?

🔊 Audio 28

1 According to forecasts by the US-based Pew Research Centre, the proportion of the British population calling itself Christian will reduce by almost a third by 2050. It will stand at just 45.4 per cent, compared with almost two thirds in 2010.

2 At the same time the number of Muslims in Britain is predicted to 5 more than double to 11.3 per cent, or one in nine of the total population.

3 But the report predicts that the biggest change will be a major expansion in the number of non-religious people. Atheists could account for just under 39 per cent, challenging Christians as the biggest faith community in the UK. 10

4 The predictions point to the most significant religious realignment in Britain since the arrival of Christianity. It would mean that by 2050 Britain would have the third largest Muslim community in Europe, as a share of the population.

5 Prof Linda Woodhead, an expert in the sociology of religion based at 15 Lancaster University, said: "The same rate of de-christianisation is not projected for Norway, Denmark, Sweden for example. So the national Church of England and Church of Scotland, seem to have been particularly effective in generating 'no religion'."

6 Terry Sanderson, president of the National Secular Society, said: 20 "Britain is still one of the most compassionate and peaceful nations in the world. In countries where religion dominates, on the other hand, there seems to be nothing but conflict and bloodshed. The fading of religion from British life is no tragedy. It might be the making of us."

NOTES   l. 9: **challenge** 挑む、競り合う   l. 14: **share of ...** ～に対する割合   l. 19: **generate** ～を生む、～ を起こす   l. 20: **secular** 世俗の   l. 21: **compassionate** 思いやりのある、情け深い

Comprehension Questions

Choose the best answer (a-c).

1. What is the Pew Research Centre?
   a. It is a British organization that conducts research into social attitudes.
   b. It is an American organization that encourages people to be less Christian.
   c. It is an organization that finds out how people are thinking on certain social subjects.

2. What is the situation with the percentage of Christians in Britain?
   a. The percentage of Christians has fallen in Britain since 2010.
   b. The reduction in the percentage of Christians in Britain is largely due to the rise in Muslims.
   c. The percentage of Christians is about 70%, compared to 2010.

3. What will the situation be concerning the increase of Muslims in Britain over the next 30 years?
   a. The number of Muslims will increase by about 11%.
   b. There will be twice the number of Muslims.
   c. Nine out of ten of the population will be Muslim.

4. What will happen to the number of non-religious people in the UK?
   a. The numbers will decline by 39%.
   b. They will become the largest faith group.
   c. The percentage will increase to nearly 40%.

5. What is the big religious change that is happening in Britain now?
   a. The decline of Christianity and the rise of other faiths.
   b. The increasing number of people who don't believe in science.
   c. The rise in the number of Muslims making Islam the major faith.

6. What will happen by 2050?
   a. There will be more Muslims in Britain than the rest of Europe.
   b. As a share of the population there will be more Muslims than Christians.
   c. Proportionally, Britain will have one of the largest Muslim populations in Europe.

7. What is Professor Woodhead's prediction concerning Christians in Northern European countries and the UK?
   a. Northern European countries will see a smaller decline in their Christian population.
   b. Northern European countries will attract more Muslims than the UK.
   c. Northern European countries will see a growth in Christians in their populations.

T/F Questions

Circle T or F for each of the following statements.

1. Professor Woodhead's remark about 'no religion' is ironic. (**T** / **F**)

2. Terry Sanderson thinks that Britain will suffer as religion declines. (**T** / **F**)

3. Terry Sanderson thinks that religious belief makes the world more peaceful and safe. (**T** / **F**)

Writing Questions

Make a full sentence, using the following words.

1. The 'faith' group with the (in the UK / in any god / the group / that / is / fastest growing membership / doesn't believe).

   _____

2. In three decades time (in Britain / 10% of / account for / the Muslim population / the population / will / more than).

   _____

© Anne Richard / Shutterstock.com
Young homeless man and his dog sitting on the street in a sleeping bag

Listening

🔊 Audio 29

Listen to the following 'Reading 2'. Fill in the correct phrase in each blank (a-e) and match the definitions below.

a. _____ b. _____ c. _____

d. _____ e. _____

1. having somewhere to live
2. to state who or what helped you
3. to be put in a place for punishment
4. one member of a family physically hurts another
5. not any more
6. to do something which is extreme
7. double the amount of...

Reading 2 — Being Homeless

1 "Shelter", a charity for the homeless, reported that 320,000 people were homeless in the UK in 2018 and 726 people died homeless. One third of homeless women cited **(a)** (DV) as the reason for being on the streets.

5 **2** Drug related homeless deaths rose by 55% compared to 2017 and at the same time 60% of local governments cut their budgets for addiction services. Such austerity hurts the poor, addicted, mentally ill, and abused.

3 The present prime minister of the UK, Boris Johnson, tweeted in 10 2009 when he was Mayor of London, 'It's scandalous that in 21st century London people have to resort to sleeping on the streets'. Less than a decade later 2018-19 figures showed 8,855 people were sleeping rough, over **(b)** of 2009-2010.

4 Until recently John Dolan was homeless and a heroin addict. By 15 2009 he had been **(c)** for a total of 12 years. He began to draw, sitting with his dog George on a London high street, selling his drawings to passers-by. Then his drawings were included in an art book and successful exhibitions of his work were held in 2013 and 2014. He is **(d)** homeless and has stopped using drugs. He credits his success to the help he got from George. His book *John and George: The Dog Who Changed* 20 *my Life* was published in 2014.

5 To solve the problem of homelessness, a social housing program "Housing First" was started. It has been successful in getting people **(e)** in such diverse places as Finland and New York.

NOTES   l. 2: **die ...**（〜として）死ぬ l. 7: **austerity** 緊縮財政 l. 11: **resort to**〔最後の手段として〕〜することに訴える、たよる l. 17: **include** 収録する、盛り込む l. 19: **credit ... to ~** …は〜のおかげだとを信じている l. 24: **diverse** 多様な

Comprehension Questions

Choose the best answer (a-c).

1. Shelter reported that in the UK in 2018...
   a. there were just under a quarter of a million homeless people.
   b. there were nearly a third of a million homeless people.
   c. there were around half a million homeless people.

2. A lot of women said they were homeless...
   a. because they didn't have enough money to rent somewhere.
   b. because the people they lived with were violent to them.
   c. because they had to live separately from their children.

3. The decision by local governments to reduce funds to addiction services...
   a. coincided with a sharp increase in deaths from drug use among the homeless.
   b. was taken at the same time as more homeless people were giving up drugs.
   c. led to an increase among people becoming homeless.

4. Cutting back on money for government spending...
   a. mainly affects people who are vulnerable.
   b. means that most people in the community suffer equally.
   c. tends to help those who need it more than others.

5. Despite Boris Johnson's tweet about the unacceptable homeless situation...
   a. the number of homeless people declined dramatically after 10 years.
   b. 10 years later there were few homeless people on the streets.
   c. there were many more homeless people 10 years later.

6. By 2009 John Dolan...

   a. was serving 12 years in prison.

   b. had served 12 years in prison.

   c. had left prison 12 years earlier.

7. He started using his talents by...

   a. drawing pictures of passers by and selling them.

   b. selling his drawings to passers by.

   c. getting George to draw pictures for sale to passers by.

T/F Questions

Circle T or F for each of the following statements.

1. John published an art book of his own paintings. (**T** / **F**)

2. He is now off the streets and lives a life free of drugs. (**T** / **F**)

3. "Housing First" is a charity that helps homeless people find a place to live.
   (**T** / **F**)

Writing Questions

Make a full sentence, using the following words.

1. John Dolan was a drug (and homeless / recognized / he was / an artist / until / addict / as).

   _____

2. The number of homeless people is increasing in Britain, (the big / a growing / in / and is / particularly / social problem / cities,).

   _____

Chapter 15

Class & Money

© James Hime
A luxurious Rolls Royce Silver Spirit, four door saloon car

階級制とお金

> 階級制度は長い歴史を持つ。王室を頂点とし下層階級までに至る。最近の上流階級にはビジネスや結婚により一代で富を得た「ニュー・リッチ」が含まれる。英国は豊かな国であるが、貧しい人も多い。富を築くことと、その富を分け合うことは別物なのだ。

Reading 1 ▶ ## Warm-up

Using your dictionary, find the meanings of the following words.

1. unemployed   2. category   3. barrister   4. wealth

5. status   6. fixed   7. nevertheless   8. class-ridden

Choose the best answer (a-c).

1. What does 'class' mean in this text?
   a. The quality of goods in the shops
   b. People being taught in a room
   c. Divisions of people in society

2. The class system exists in Britain to...
   a. encourage people to improve their status.
   b. organize people in society.
   c. give people a feeling of history.

Reading 1 What is the British Class System?

🔊 Audio 30

1 Before the Industrial Revolution British society was clearly divided into groups. People's membership of a group depended on what kind of family they were born into. The present class system can be divided into five main groups.

5 **2** The underclass consists of the long-term unemployed or homeless people. The working class is made up of those with no higher education who work on production lines in factories or as labourers.

3 The majority of British people fall into the middle class category, which includes shop owners, white-collar workers, teachers, journalists,
10 nurses and so on. People with a high paying career such as barristers can be considered upper class. The tiny group composed of the royal family and titled people are called aristocrats.

4 Wealth can push a person into the upper class. Such people are often called 'new money'. 'Old money' refers to people with title and of
15 aristocratic birth. However, ancient English families still maintain high social status even if they are no longer wealthy.

5 And class is not always fixed. For example, when Kate Middleton married Prince William her upper middle class lifestyle was quickly boosted into aristocratic class status.

20 **6** The class system in today's society doesn't have the same meaning as it once did. Working class people can become middle or upper class by gaining a good education and going into a profession or by acquiring wealth. Nevertheless, as George Orwell, the famous author, said, Britain is "the most class-ridden society under the sun" and class is still
25 alive and well in modern Britain.

NOTES   l. 3: **<be> born into** ～に生まれる   l. 8: **fall into** ～に分類される   l. 9: **white-collar worker** 事務の仕事をしている人   l. 12: **aristocrat** 貴族階級の人   l. 13: **push ~ into** （人）を～するように後押しする、押し上げる   l. 24: **under the sun** 地球上で、世界中で

Comprehension Questions

Choose the best answer (a-c).

1. What is the main factor that decides which class British people become part of?

   a. The family they are born into

   b. The way their parents speak

   c. The effect of the Industrial Revolution

2. How would you describe somebody with little or no income who receives welfare payments?

   a. This person belongs to the working class.

   b. This person belongs to the under class.

   c. This person belongs to the middle class.

3. What is the main condition that shows someone is in the upper class?

   a. Having a regular income

   b. Having the right to wear a white collar at work

   c. Having a high-level, high paying career position

4. What is the main way to get into the upper class quickly?

   a. By making a lot of money

   b. By making friends with top people

   c. By telling everyone that you are upper class

5. How would you categorize someone who has been rich for generations?

   a. Such a person is called 'old money.'

   b. Such a person is called 'new money.'

   c. Such a person is called 'middle class.'

6. What are the three factors that decide the class that people belong to?

   a. Birth, title and contacts

   b. Title, friends and family

   c. Money, title and family

7. What does the phrase "class-ridden society" mean?

   a. A country where classy aristocrats ride horses

   b. A nation of fashionable people with class

   c. A class system which damages the nation

T/F Questions

1. There are poor aristocrats who maintain their status in society. (**T** / **F**)

2. Most people in Britain are members of the lower class. (**T** / **F**)

3. The class system is more flexible nowadays than in the past. (**T** / **F**)

Writing Questions

Make a full sentence, using the following words.

1. One's position (partly to / system / in the class / birth / do with / is / in Britain) but nowadays is more about money.

   _____

2. Some people in (believe / belong to / the class system / the UK / they / a certain group / within), even if their belief does not fit the reality of their situation.

   _____

© Elena Rostunova

© Steve Gill Photography

Listen to the following 'Reading 2'. Fill in the correct phrase in each blank (a-e) and match the definitions below.

a. _____ b. _____ c. _____

d. _____ e. _____

1. a point in the future
2. things that people own
3. giving other people things
4. anticipate some future event
5. the agreed price of something
6. to have a skill or ability
7. This happens when some people are richer than others

Reading 2   How Wealthy are the British?

1 The UK is wealthy. Total wealth is estimated at almost 13 trillion pounds. In the 1960s the value of property, pensions and savings was about three times GDP. Now it is nearly seven times GDP. Property **(a)** 4.6tn pounds while pensions are worth 5.3tn pounds. Financial wealth (stocks and shares etc.) is worth 1.6tn pounds while physical wealth is 5 probably around 1.2tn pounds. Britons own 4.3bn pound's worth of personalized number plates, for example.

2 The richest tenth of families in the UK have around 670,000 pounds per adult, excluding personal possessions. The bottom tenth of families have less than 3 pounds per adult. Even though there is **(b)**, the share of 10 wealth of the richest 1% in the country fell for most of the 20th century and hasn't changed much since.

3 Some millennials, those aged 19-38, can **(c)** a large inheritance income from their parents. On the other hand, because longevity is increasing, they will be in their 60s **(d)** they can enjoy it. But they are 15 luckier than those who have no expectation of inheritance.

4 Additionally, there is a wealth gap between the young and old–those in their 60s are the richest-and between the poorer north and the richer south of England, including London.

20 **5** The size and distribution of wealth matters because it affects the economy and society. Those without any wealth face poverty. Britain has **(e)** growing wealth but not so good at sharing it out.

NOTES　　l. 4: **tn = trillion** 1 兆　l. 5: **stock**〔一社の全体の〕株、株式　l. 5: **share**〔売買の単位としての〕株、株式　l. 6: **bn = billion** 10 億　l. 13: **inheritance** 遺産

Comprehension Questions

　Choose the best answer (a-c).

1. What has happened to Britain's wealth over the last fifty years?
   a. It has slowly risen over time.
   b. It has increased by more than double.
   c. It has expanded to over 13tn pounds.

2. Which is the largest portion of Britain's total wealth?
   a. The largest is pensions at 42% of the total.
   b. The largest is property at 4.6tn pounds.
   c. The largest is physical wealth.

3. What is the true situation of wealth distribution?
   a. The top tenth of the population is 200,000 times richer than the bottom tenth.
   b. The richest have increased their wealth thousands of times during the 20th century.
   c. Those at the bottom of the wealth rankings still have considerable savings.

4. Some millennials...
   a. cannot wait for their parents to die.
   b. will be able to benefit from wealth left by their parents.
   c. are too old to receive an inheritance.

5. Those millennials who receive an inheritance...
   a. will be dead by the time they get it.
   b. will be expecting more than they get.
   c. will be luckier than others who don't.

6. Who are likely to be the wealthiest in the UK?

   a. Those who are in their 60s and live in the north

   b. Those who live in London and who are young

   c. Those near retirement age who live in the south

7. As far as wealth is concerned the British have been successful in...

   a. increasing the general amount of wealth.

   b. reducing the difference between rich and poor.

   c. sharing wealth equally in society.

T/F Questions

Circle T or F for each of the following statements.

1. Adults in the richest 10% of the population have wealth of over half a million pounds. (**T** / **F**)

2. People born after 1980 are likely to inherit wealth from their parents. (**T** / **F**)

3. Britain is one of the poorest nations in the world. (**T** / **F**)

Writing Questions

Make a full sentence, using the following words.

1. Britain is better at (in distributing / fairly / the population / wealth creation / wealth / among / than).

   _____

2. Wealthy British people make (or close relatives / a will / to their children / and leave / and possessions / property / their money,), before they die.

   _____